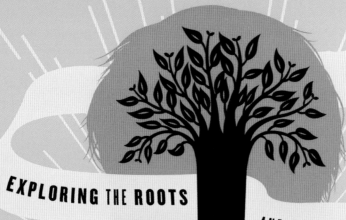

EXPLORING THE ROOTS AND SHOOTS OF FAITH

THE **RADICAL BOOK** FOR KIDS

CHAMP THORNTON

New Growth Press, Greensboro, NC 27404
Copyright © 2016 by George Thomas Thornton II

Unless otherwise indicated, Scripture quotations are taken from *The Holy Bible, English Standard Version.* Copyright © 2000; 2001 by Crossway Bibles, a division of Good News Publishers. Used by permission. All rights reserved.

Scripture quotations marked NIV are taken from THE HOLY BIBLE, NEW INTERNATIONAL VERSION®, NIV® Copyright © 1973, 1978, 1984, 2011 by Biblica, Inc.® Used by permission. All rights reserved worldwide.

Scripture quotations marked NLT are taken from the Holy Bible, New Living Translation, copyright ©1996, 2004, 2007 by Tyndale House Foundation. Used by permission of Tyndale House Publishers, Inc., Carol Stream, Illinois 60188. All rights reserved.

Scripture taken from *The Message*. Copyright © 1993, 1994, 1995, 1996, 2000, 2001, 2002. Used by permission of NavPress Publishing Group.

Cover Design: Faceout Books, faceoutstudio.com
Interior Design and Typesetting: Scot McDonald
See back of book for sources and illustration credits.

ISBN 978-1-942572-71-8 (Print)
ISBN 978-1-942572-70-1 (eBook)

Library of Congress Cataloging-in-Publication Data

Names: Thornton, George, 1973- author.
Title: The radical book for kids : exploring the roots and shoots of faith /
    George "Champ" Thornton.
Description: Greensboro, NC : New Growth Press, 2016. | Includes
    bibliographical references.
Identifiers: LCCN 2016007198 | ISBN 9781942572718 (hardcover)
Subjects: LCSH: Christianity—Juvenile literature.
Classification: LCC BR125.5 .T46 2016 | DDC 230—dc23
LC record available at https://lccn.loc.gov/2016007198

Printed in China

23 22 21 20 19 18 17 16   1 2 3 4 5

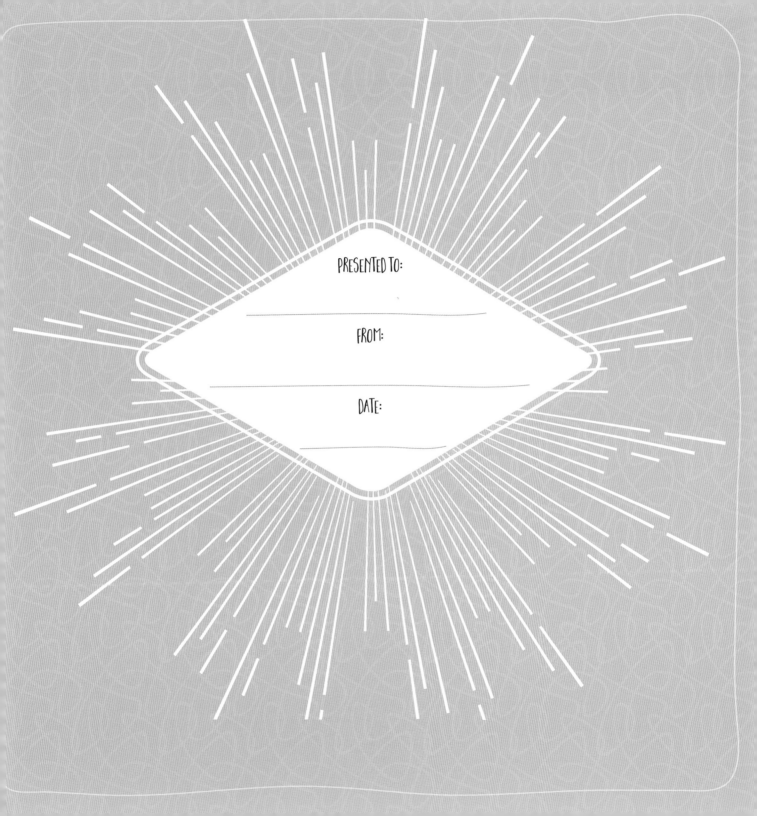

PRESENTED TO:

_____

FROM:

_____

DATE:

_____

For Shannon

Brother, friend, and ally for the next generation

All that is gold does not glitter,
Not all those who wander are lost;
The old that is strong does not wither,
Deep roots are not reached by the frost.

—*J. R. R. Tolkien*, The Fellowship of the Ring

CONTENTS

A Word of Explanation for Adults

I wrote this book for a reason—three of them actually (two boys and a girl). My three children are right now between the ages of six and eleven, but one day they'll be grownups, and perhaps have families of their own.

As parents, we all want what is best for the next generation—that they will love, trust, and follow the Lord Jesus Christ. So it's my prayer that this book will be used by God to grow deep roots of faith in the children who read it.

More than this, I hope that it will also encourage young readers to keep on learning about his Word, his gospel, his church, and life in his world. If this book makes our children more curious and thirsty to know God and the good news of his Word, then it will have done its job.

The Radical Book for Kids is intended for children, ages 8–14, to read on their own. But parents or teachers may also find it helpful as a supplement for devotions or discussions. Whatever its use, may this book—like an assorted packet of seeds—fall into good soil, take root, grow up, and bear fruit—all to the praise of the Gardener.

"And now I commend you to God and to the word of his grace, which is able to build you up. . . ." (Acts 20:32a).

WARNING: YOU HOLD IN YOUR HANDS A *RADICAL* BOOK.

Did you know that the word *radical* has a few different meanings? Originally it meant "going to the root" of something. So—*if you dare*—this book will take you *deep* into the ancient roots of our faith. You'll learn about God's Word—what it teaches, why you should trust it, and how you can live it. As you grow up, you should also grow *down*—letting the Bible sink its roots deep into your heart.

Radical also means "extreme, drastic, revolutionary." If a tree has a good root system, it can stand the wildest storms. So in this book, you'll learn about following Jesus and standing for him in the storms of life. You'll also meet people who did the same even when everything seemed against them. How did they do it? God gave them radical faith.

You'll also find radical ("excellent, cool") fun. You'll read about ancient weapons, create pottery, discover ancient languages, locate stars, play a board game that's 3,000 years old—and more.

So, read this book any way you'd like: skip around, or read straight through. But remember: all the roots of our faith grow out of The Tree. The one on which Jesus died in the place of sinners. May everything you read point you to him: the radical Rescuer of rebels.

THE BIBLE IN ONE SENTENCE

I f someone quizzed you: "Please state the message of the entire Bible in one sentence," what would you say? Not an easy job, is it? After all, the Bible comprises 1,189 chapters divided into 66 different sections or "books." How do you cram all that into a single sentence?

You can't fit everything in. But what if all 66 books fit together like chapters in a story? Then you might try to summarize that story. Now we're getting somewhere.

So, what big story does the Bible tell? One way to learn something about a story is to read the beginning and the ending. Stories are like houses: the best way to get in is usually through the front door or the back door.

What do the Bible's beginning (Genesis) and ending (Revelation) reveal about the story of the entire Bible? What connections do you notice (see chart)?

In the beginning God made the world, and he made it all "very good" (Genesis 1:31). But it didn't take long for people to ruin what he had created. But at the end of the story, God will set everything right once more.

IN THE BEGINNING...

AT THE ENDING...

IN THE BEGINNING...	AT THE ENDING...
DAY & NIGHT ARE CREATED (Gen. 1:5)	**NO MORE NIGHT** (Rev. 22:5)
THE WORLD IS MADE (Gen. 1–2)	**THE WORLD IS MADE NEW** (Rev. 21:1)
TREE OF LIFE MADE (Gen. 2:9)	**TREE OF LIFE CONTINUES** (Rev. 22:2)
GOD DWELLS WITH PEOPLE (Gen. 3:8)	**GOD AGAIN DWELLS WITH PEOPLE** (Rev. 21:3)
PEOPLE DISOBEY GOD (Gen. 3:6)	**PEOPLE OBEY GOD** (Rev. 21:27)
PEOPLE BEGIN FIGHTING EACH OTHER (Gen. 3:12)	**PEOPLE STOP FIGHTING EACH OTHER** (Rev. 21:24-26)
SICKNESS AND DEATH ENTER THE WORLD (Gen. 3:19)	**SICKNESS AND DEATH CONQUERED** (Rev. 22:4)
SATAN (THE SERPENT) DESTROYS (Gen. 3:1)	**SATAN DEFEATED** (Rev. 20:2, 10)

So what *connects* the start with the finish? The story that fills the middle is all about Jesus. The Old Testament looks ahead and prepares for his coming. The New Testament looks back and explains his coming. The story of the Bible is the story of Jesus and why he came to earth.

"GOD MADE IT, WE BROKE IT, JESUS FIXES IT."
Michael Williams

The Bible teaches that Jesus came with this mission: to make everything new again. Everything that sin had wrecked, he came to repair.

And that brings us back to where we started. How to sum up the Bible in one sentence? Here's one attempt. The story of the Bible is that . . . **Through Jesus, God is restoring everything that sin ruined.**

Can you think of any areas in your life that seem messed up because of your sin or someone else's sin? The sad truth is that sin touches every part of life, which makes quite a mess. And it's impossible to do much to fix our *own* lives. But nothing is too hard for Jesus. He loves to fix broken things.

After all, the whole Bible reminds us that Jesus came to restore all things.

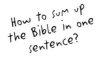

How to sum up the Bible in one sentence?

MORE TO EXPLORE

If you'd like to learn more about the story of the Bible, you may want to read *Grandpa's Box* by Starr Meade.

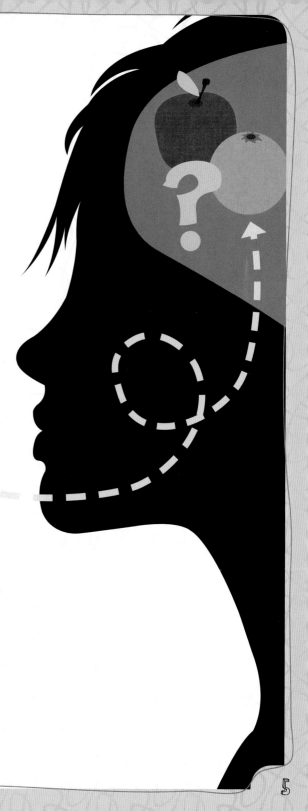

HOW TO UNDERSTAND THE BIBLE

he Bible tells one big story. But if you've spent any time reading it, you already know it's not like most two-thousand-page books that you can check out of the library. Instead, God's Word is more like the *library itself*: in it are many different kinds of books—poetry, letters, history, and more. Each part of the Bible has its own style.

So if you are going to understand what is written in the Bible, you must also know *how* it's written.

We all know that how something is put together changes the way you work with it. Oranges have rinds, and apples have cores, so you eat them differently— one, you peel; the other, you core. The same is true of books. If a story starts with the phrase, "Once upon a time," you know it's a fairy tale and that you don't read it like a history book.

The Bible is no different. If you're going to understand the Bible, you need to know the kinds of literature it contains. Then you can read them each in the right way. These different kinds or styles are called *genres*.

But why couldn't God just have given us a book with all the same style?

Scripture contains many genres in order to help you—all of you. You have feelings, so there are parts of his Word, for example, the poetry of Psalms, that speak to your heart. You have thoughts, so there are letters, like Romans, that stretch your mind. You make choices, so there are Bible commands that challenge your obedience. Most of all, we learn from stories, so the Bible tells us many true stories (and of course all of them fit into the one true story about Jesus rescuing the world from death and evil). God's Word speaks personally to every part of your life.

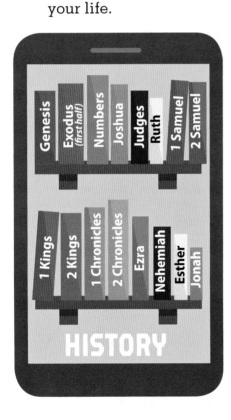

Here's a basic list of genres in the Bible. (The bookshelves show which individual books of the Bible fit into which genres.)

History—The entire Bible is historically true, and about one-half of the Old Testament focuses on retelling historical events. They recount what God has done for his people: he made them, loves them, leads them, forgives them, etc. None of his people deserves any of his kindness. All his people, even the best of the kings, are filled with weakness and often fail. This means that the hero of these stories is God himself. And the Old Testament tells how one day God will send the perfect King to rescue his flawed and failing people.

Law—Right in the middle of the stories, God tells his people how he wants them to live. He is their authority. As their true King, God gives them rules that show what he loves, what he hates, and what will be best for them. Yet God's people can't obey perfectly. So they need forgiveness. And years after the Law was written, God would send Someone who always obeyed God's Law, the perfect Sacrifice for sin.

Poetry—Over one-third of the Bible is poetry. Instead of having rhyming sounds, poems in the Bible have rhyming ideas that combine to make one beautiful point. (For example, the first line of Psalm 9:9 says, *"The LORD is a refuge for the oppressed."* The second line of this poem matches and builds on the first: *"[The LORD is] a stronghold in times of trouble."* [NIV]) The biblical authors wrote in this kind of poetry to express their feelings to God—sometimes in songs, sad or happy, but always from the heart. God has promised to set everything right one day. And that promise puts every song into the key of hope!

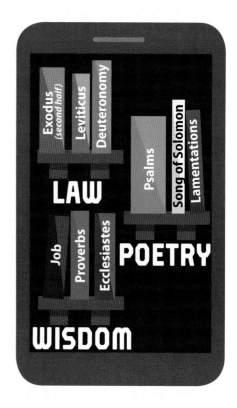

Wisdom—A handful of Old Testament books teach how to live skillfully (wisely) before God in this wonderful, painful, and complicated world. These books, like Proverbs, often recognize that life usually follows certain God-created patterns; for example, if you do wrong, you will usually get caught.

They also remind us that wisdom comes from trusting God. None of us can do that perfectly and that's why God would eventually send the wisest Man ever, who always trusted God with his whole heart.

What is the longest book in the Bible?

(Answer: Psalms has the most verses [2,527] and chapters [150], but Jeremiah has the most letters [over 41,000 of them])

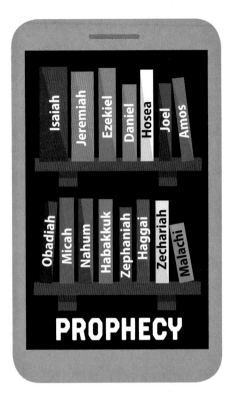

PROPHECY

Isaiah Jeremiah Ezekiel Daniel Hosea Joel Amos

Obadiah Micah Nahum Habakkuk Zephaniah Haggai Zechariah Malachi

Prophecy—These books mostly record the sermons of the prophets God sent to deliver his messages to his sinful people. Sometimes the prophets spoke about what God would do in the future (they would foretell). And sometimes they would simply preach to God's people (they would forth-tell).

In these messages the prophets encouraged God's people by reminding them that God still loved them. The prophets also warned God's people to forsake their sin and turn back to God. If they refused, bad things would happen. In light of all this sin, one day God would send the perfect Person who would do for God's people what they never could do—obey and love God perfectly.

Gospels and Acts—The four Gospels report on the life, death, and resurrection of Jesus Christ. They feature eyewitness testimonies from people who were actually there. They record how Jesus set the perfect example and gave commands to be obeyed. Yet the good news of the Gospels (*gospel* means "good news") is that Jesus Christ lived and died, not merely as an example or teacher, but as our substitute. He was the One for whom

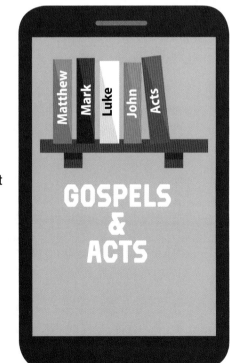

GOSPELS & ACTS

Matthew Mark Luke John Acts

God's people had been waiting. Jesus lived the life we could never live, and died the death we should have died. The book of Acts follows the Gospels and continues the story of Jesus, telling how the good news spread all over the world.

Letters—The letters (also known as *epistles*) of the New Testament help explain the importance of Jesus's life, death, and resurrection. What was the meaning of all God had done through Jesus? The truth in these letters helps God's people deal with temptation, error, and suffering.

Apocalyptic Literature—This genre focuses on revealing the future. ("Apocalyptic" comes from a Greek word meaning "to reveal.") In this kind of book, it's not always easy to understand the details of what will happen in the future. The writing is often mysterious. But what's crystal clear is that no matter how bad things get, no matter how much the world hates God and his people, Jesus will triumph! The story of the Bible—and the story of the world—will have a happy ending!

Remember: sometimes you will find several genres inside a single book of the Bible. For example, Exodus contains history, law, and poetry. So, in order to simplify, the books of Scripture are matched up with the category of literature they feature most.

LETTERS

Romans
1 Corinthians
2 Corinthians
Galatians
Ephesians
Philippians
Colossians
1 Thessalonians
2 Thessalonians
1 Timothy
2 Timothy

Titus
Philemon
Hebrews
James
1 Peter
2 Peter
1 John
2 John
3 John
Jude

APOCALYPTIC LITERATURE

Daniel
Revelation of John

3

NAMES OF GOD

In the Bible, God is known by many names. They're not just what he's called; they're what he's *like* (Psalm 68:4). Some names are straightforward, like "God" or "Jesus." Others are compound names, like "God Almighty" (Revelation 19:15) or "Lord Most High" (Genesis 14:22). Still other names are more like a description: "Holy One" (Isaiah 40:25), or "One Enthroned in Heaven" (Psalm 2:4), "The Mighty One" (Isaiah 1:4), or "The Righteous One" (Isaiah 24:1).

All of these names of God are like windows through which you can look and learn about him.

MORE TO EXPLORE If you'd like to learn more about the names of God, you may want to read *God's Names (Making Him Known)* by Sally Michael.

ANCIENT OF DAYS
The King has always existed and reigns from his mighty throne.
Daniel 7:9

JESUS
Jehovah saves. God to the rescue!
Matthew 1:21

CHRIST
Messiah, anointed one
Matthew 11:12

GOD
The most common name for the Lord, Hebrew, *elohim*
Deuteronomy 32:4

LORD
Master or King,
Hebrew *adonai*

Exodus 34:9

LORD
Using all capital
letters, this is the name
Jehovah (or Yahweh), the
name God uses with
his own people

Exodus 20:2

YAHWEH SABAOTH
The LORD of
Hosts (Armies)

Isaiah 13:4

YAHWEH JIREH
The LORD Provides

Genesis 22:14

EL OLAM
Everlasting God

Genesis 21:33

YAHWEH ROPHE
The LORD your Healer

Exodus 15:26

EL ELYON
God Most High

Psalm 73:11

YAHWEH ZEDEK
The LORD our
Righteousness

Jeremiah 23:5-6

EL ROI
The God who Sees

Genesis 16:13

EL SHADDAI
God Almighty

Genesis 28:3

Which book of the Bible doesn't mention God once?
(Answer: Esther)

11

4

GREAT NEWS!

What do you think it means to be a Christian?

- ☐ A. I'm a nice person
- ☐ B. I go to church on Sunday
- ☐ C. I try to obey God and obey my parents
- ☐ D. I read my Bible and pray almost every day
- ☐ E. None of the above

Sometimes when you ask people, "Do you want to become a Christian?" they reply, "I'm not ready. There are parts of my life I need to fix first. Then I'll become a Christian."

This person thinks that being a Christian means you have to be good enough and obey the Bible more. They think Christianity is all about following the good advice Jesus gave. But they're wrong. At its heart, Christianity is not good advice; it's good news.

Here's the difference.

Advice tells you something that would be good to do. It has not happened yet.

News tells you something that *has already* happened. There is nothing you can do about it.

Here's an example: Pretend that you lived in a castle in the days of knights and kingdoms. One day an enemy king invades, marching his army into your kingdom. So your king gathers his army and goes out to meet the enemy on the field of battle, miles from the castle. And now you and everyone in the castle await word from the battlefield: Did the king win or lose?

If your king has lost, he will send back soldiers who will give *advice* about how to prepare the castle for enemy invasion. You and the other citizens will get ready to fight for your lives. You will set up extra protection and weapons, but will it be enough? Fear and dread fill every heart.

But, if your king has won, he will send back messengers who will announce the wonderful *news* of the victory. You and the rest of the citizens in the castle can enjoy normal and active lives. Joy and peace fill every heart.

You see, Christianity announces the greatest news in the history of the universe: the gospel of Jesus Christ. He has already come to earth and completely defeated all our enemies: sin, death, and Satan. The battle has been fought and won. There's nothing for you to do, except live your lives in joy and peace, relying on the

"Gospel" means good news. The modern English word comes from the Old English, "gōd-spel" (gōd = good; spel = news or story). This word is a translation of the Greek word, evangelion, which literally means "good news."

victory he has already accomplished.

In other words, this gospel is the announcement that through the life, death, and resurrection of King Jesus, God is setting everything right again, including the men and women who are repenting and relying on this King as their only Rescuer from sin.

By now it should be clear that Christianity is not a religion that's a list of advice for you to do. No, instead Christianity brings news of what Jesus has already *done*. It's not about the accomplishment of your good works; it's about the announcement of *his* good works.

∅   ∅   ∅

So, how will you respond to this great news? There are only two ways.

1. **You can reject your King and Rescuer, Jesus Christ, and try to live life according to your rules and save yourself.** This kind of person can look either bad or good by the world's standards. It doesn't matter which: both reject Jesus.

2. **Or you can live with Jesus Christ as your King and Rescuer.** Turn from living as your own king (repent) and trust in Jesus for rescue (faith).

The second kind of person does bad things, as well as good things. But most importantly, this person has been rescued by King Jesus—from both her own badness and goodness. That's what a Christian is. And that's great news!

FOR EVERYONE HAS SINNED; WE ALL FALL SHORT OF GOD'S GLORIOUS STANDARD. YET GOD, IN HIS GRACE, FREELY MAKES US RIGHT IN HIS SIGHT. HE DID THIS THROUGH CHRIST JESUS WHEN HE FREED US FROM THE PENALTY FOR OUR SINS. FOR GOD PRESENTED JESUS AS THE SACRIFICE FOR SIN. PEOPLE ARE MADE RIGHT WITH GOD WHEN THEY BELIEVE THAT JESUS SACRIFICED HIS LIFE, SHEDDING HIS BLOOD.
ROMANS 3:23–25A NLT

5

HOW TO GROW AS A CHRISTIAN

A fter you become a Christian, God wants you to *grow* as a Christian. This growing looks like trusting and obeying Jesus more and more. And this kind of growth is challenging: more like growing muscles than growing flowers. If it were easy, all of God's people would be strong, mature believers (and you wouldn't need to read this chapter).

But Christian growth is *not* easy; it takes work. It's not quick; it takes time. And it's never finished; it continues your whole life.

Thankfully, God does more than just tell you to grow, he also provides the help you need to grow. Some of these resources for growth are called "habits of grace" or "spiritual disciplines."

What are Spiritual Disciplines?
They are practices "that promote spiritual

PRAYER

GOD'S WORD

Talk with other Christians about what God is teaching you. Hebrews 3:13

SHARING

CONFESSION
("I have sinned, forgive in mercy")
Daniel 9:4–6

READ
the Bible every day
1 Timothy 4:13

SHARE
Where you've seen God at work
Acts 14:27

PRAISE
("I worship you for who you are")
Psalm 139:14

THINK OFTEN
about God's Word
Psalm 1:1–3

SHARE
Where you're struggling
Galatians 6:2

THANKSGIVING
("I thank you for what you've done")
Psalm 118:21

LISTEN CAREFULLY
to the Word of God preached and taught
1 Thess 2:13

SHARE
Where you're tempted
James 5:16

Keep practicing these "spiritual disciplines"—giving your attention to the Word and prayer. This practice won't make you perfect, but over time God will help you grow. He'll strengthen you to rely more on Jesus for everything you need, and to act more like Jesus in everything you do. This is how a Christian grows.

AFFIRMATION
("I rehearse what is true about you")
Psalm 27:1–3

MEMORIZE GOD'S WORD
Psalm 119:11

PETITION
("I ask you for what is needed")
Matthew 6:11

17

Did You KNOW ?

Christians keep growing their entire life. Charles Simeon was a pastor in London for 53 years, from 1783 to 1836. He was known as a godly man who loved God's Word, but he wasn't always that way.

He didn't become a Christian until in college, and even after he became a pastor he continued to struggle with controlling his temper.

Once while visiting Henry Venn and his family, Pastor Simeon responded harshly to another man. Mr. Venn's daughters saw it all.

After Pastor Simeon left, Mr. Venn took his daughters into their garden, and asked them to pick a young peach for him. When his girls asked why their father wanted a peach that had not yet ripened, he said, "Well, my dears, it is green now, and we must wait; but a little more sun, and a few more showers, and the peach will be ripe and sweet. So it is with Mr. Simeon."

And so it is with all of us who seek—through the sunshine and showers of the spiritual disciplines—to keep growing as Christians.

growth. They are the habits of devotion we should use, with the Holy Spirit's help, in the pursuit of Godliness."

❧ ❧ ❧

Keep practicing these "spiritual disciplines"— giving your attention to the Word and prayer. This practice won't make you perfect, but over time God will help you grow. He'll strengthen you to rely more on Jesus for everything you need, and to act more like Jesus in everything you do. This is how a Christian grows.

6

MEN WHO GAVE THEIR LIVES FOR CHRIST

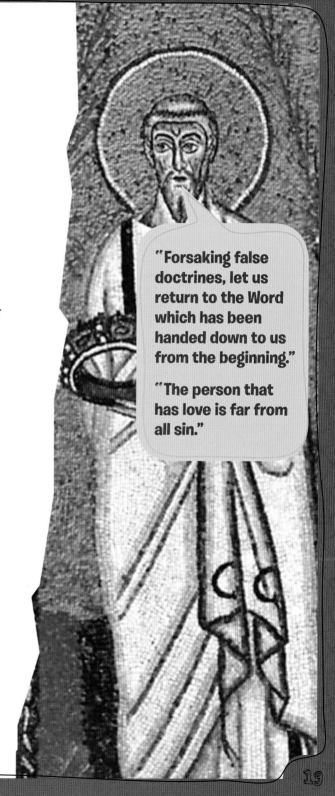

Polycarp was born around A.D. 70 and died around A.D. 160. He became a Christian under the ministry of none other than the apostle John! For fifty years Polycarp served as a godly pastor in Smyrna, a city in Asia Minor (modern day Turkey). Around A.D. 156, the Roman government in the area around Smyrna began persecuting Christians. Rome declared that if Christians would say that the Roman emperor was "lord," they could go free. If they refused, they would be killed. When faced with this choice, Polycarp said: "For eighty-six years, I have been Christ's servant, and he has never done me wrong. How can I curse my King who saved me?" Polycarp willingly died for his Lord, Jesus Christ.

"Forsaking false doctrines, let us return to the Word which has been handed down to us from the beginning."

"The person that has love is far from all sin."

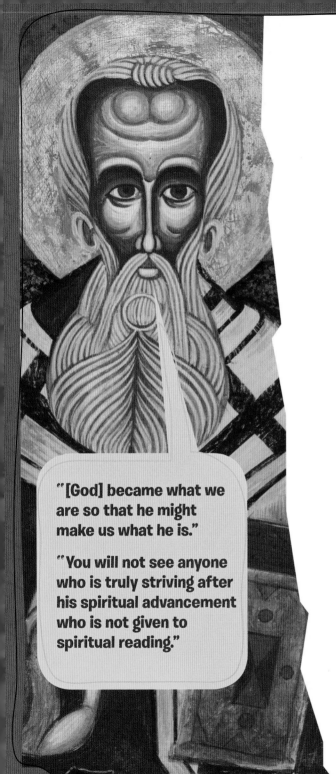

"[God] became what we are so that he might make us what he is."

"You will not see anyone who is truly striving after his spiritual advancement who is not given to spiritual reading."

Athanasius (A.D. 296–373) served as a pastor and church leader in his hometown of Alexandria, Egypt for forty-six years. During his ministry, the churches around the world were in the middle of an important debate about who Jesus is.

In that time, many pastors unfortunately followed the teaching of a pastor named Arius, who didn't believe that God is Father, Son, and Holy Spirit (this is called the doctrine of the Trinity). Arius and his followers believed that if there is (a) one God and (b) Christ is distinct from the Father, then (c) Christ cannot be God. But the Bible clearly teaches that Jesus Christ was God come in the flesh and that he sent his Spirit to be with his people after he went back to heaven—that's one God in three distinct and equally glorious Persons.

Since many church leaders believed in Arianism, they hated Athanasius and his faithfulness to the Bible's actual teaching about the Trinity. As a result, Athanasius was exiled five different times, spending seventeen years in exile far from his home and the church he loved. Once a friend exclaimed, "Athanasius, the whole world is against you!" Athanasius answered boldly:

"Then it is Athanasius against the world." This earned him the Latin nickname: *Athanasius Contra Mundum.*

Through his courageous efforts spanning forty-six years, Athanasius helped the church reclaim the Bible's true teaching about the Trinity and the identity of Jesus.

∅ ∅ ∅

REMEMBER YOUR LEADERS, THOSE WHO SPOKE TO YOU THE WORD OF GOD. CONSIDER THE OUTCOME OF THEIR WAY OF LIFE, AND IMITATE THEIR FAITH. JESUS CHRIST IS THE SAME YESTERDAY AND TODAY AND FOREVER. HEBREWS 13:7–8

∅ ∅ ∅

Augustine was born in A.D. 354 and died in 430. He was a pastor and church leader in the city of Hippo in North Africa (in modern day Algeria) for forty years. Augustine wrote more than one hundred books, many of which are still widely

Did You KNOW ?

You won't find the word "Trinity" in the Bible. But here are some Bible verses that show us how God is One, made up of three—Father, Son, and Holy Spirit:

After his baptism, as Jesus came up out of the water, the heavens were opened and he saw the Spirit of God descending like a dove and settling on him. And a voice from heaven said, "This is my dearly loved Son, who brings me great joy" (Matthew 3:16-17).

"Therefore, go and make disciples of all the nations, baptizing them in the name of the Father and the Son and the Holy Spirit" (Matthew 28:19).

May the grace of the Lord Jesus Christ, the love of God, and the fellowship of the Holy Spirit be with you all (2 Corinthians 13:14).

Here are some more verses to look up in your Bible: Deuteronomy 6:4; John 14:26; 1 Timothy 2:5.

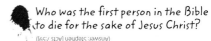

Who was the first person in the Bible to die for the sake of Jesus Christ?

(Answer: Stephen [Acts 7:59])

21

Augustine's Confessions

A masterpiece of spiritual autobiography, the **Confessions** comprises thirteen units (books). The first nine units recount events and reflections from the first forty years of Augustine's life, while the last four mostly offer his comments on theology, with special attention on the book of Genesis. Here are some prayers from the **Confessions**:

"You have made us for yourself, and our heart is restless until it rests in you." (Book 1)

"Without you, what am I to myself but a guide to my own self-destruction." (Book 4)

"I sighed and you heard me. I wavered and you steadied me. I travelled along the broad way of the world, but you did not desert me." (Book 6)

"On your exceedingly great mercy rests all my hope. Give what you command, and then command whatever you will." (Book 10)

read today—1,600 years later. Probably his most famous and beloved book is part autobiography and part theology, simply titled *Confessions*. Through his writings, Augustine remains one of the most important teachers in the history of Christ's church.

But Augustine wasn't always a faithful Christian pastor. Although he had a Christian mother, Augustine decided, when he grew up, that he would live the way *he* wanted. As a young man, Augustine ran far from God both in his beliefs and in his actions. And he was miserable in his sinful living.

Yet God graciously led Augustine to hear the gospel from a preacher named Ambrose. Augustine wrote about what happened to him not long after hearing Ambrose's preaching:

"[I was] weeping in the most bitter contrition of my heart, when, lo! I heard from a neighboring house a voice, as of a boy or girl, I know not, chanting, and often repeating, 'Take up and read; take up and read.' . . . So I arose . . . and read the first chapter I should find . . . . I seized [Paul's letter to the Romans], opened, and in silence read that section on which my eyes first fell."

This is what he read, "Don't participate in the darkness of wild parties and drunkenness, or in sexual promiscuity and immoral living, or in quarreling and jealousy. Instead, clothe yourself with the presence of the Lord Jesus Christ. And don't let yourself think about ways to indulge your evil desires" (Romans 13:13b–14 NLT).

Augustine said, "No further would I read; nor needed I: for instantly at the end of this sentence, by a light as it were of peace shone into my heart, all the darkness of doubt vanished away." And so it was that through his powerful Word, God led a straying sinner into his family and into his service.

MORE TO EXPLORE Simonetta Carr has written a book series, *"Christian Biographies for Young Readers."* In addition to her biographies about Athanasius and Augustine of Hippo, you are sure to enjoy others, for example, the ones about John Calvin and John Knox.

7

WHAT TO DO WHEN YOU'RE ANGRY

What makes you mad?

1 "My brother won't let me watch my favorite show! He makes me so angry!"

2 "My sister won't get off the computer! It really ticks me off."

3 "This schoolwork is terrible— I can't stand it!"

4 "My dad never listens to me! He's driving me crazy!"

5 "That kid at school keeps annoying me! I hate school!"

Hopefully, all of these don't make you mad. That'd be really bad news. But even if they did, there's some good news you need to hear.

Did you know that anger is not your biggest problem? Of course, it's true that God calls explosions of temper—and smoldering resentment—sin (Galatians 5:19–21). But even if you checked all those boxes, your deepest problem is not that you get upset with other people.

The real issue is the reason *why* you get angry at people. This is the sin beneath the sin— like the large part of an iceberg floating beneath the surface. The Bible teaches that you're getting mad because you're not getting what you want. Jesus's half-brother, James, puts it this way:

What is causing the quarrels and fights among you? Don't they come from the evil desires at war within you? You want what you don't have, so you scheme and kill to get it. You are jealous of what others have, but you can't get it, so you fight and wage war to take it away from them. (James 4:1–2)

Typically, the reasons you get angry are because (1) you **want** something you don't have or (2) you **lost** something you wanted to keep.

So, go back and revisit the five "What makes you mad?" boxes at the beginning of this chapter. Take some time to think about what is either **"wanted"** or **"lost"** in each of the examples.

To get you started, here's an example of what might be going on beneath the surface for **#1**.

1 **"My brother won't let me watch my favorite show! He makes me so angry!"**

I want to watch my favorite show. My brother is keeping me from getting what I want; so I am angry with him. He's going to have to pay for not giving me what I want.

What do you think might be **wanted** or **lost** for each of the other comments?

I'm Starting to Feel Angry . . .

What should you do, then, when you feel yourself starting to get angry?

Pray. Tell God that you're sorry for your attitude. Confess to God what it is that you're really wanting, and ask him for strength to keep calm. In your anger, you may want something you can't get, but in reality what you *need* is a gift that God loves to give: his help (or "grace").

Let us then with confidence draw near to the throne of grace, that we may receive mercy and find grace to help in time of need. (Hebrews 4:16)

Wait to talk. When you're mad, don't say much—or anything at all, really. Once you calm down, you might actually use your words to help the person who had made you angry. When it's the right time, you may also find it helpful to talk with the person about what made you upset.

A soft answer turns away wrath, but a harsh word stirs up anger. The tongue of the wise commends knowledge, but the mouths of fools pour out folly. (Proverbs 15:1–2)

Show love instead. Rather than getting angry at someone, God wants you to treat that person in love. When that person does something "evil," try giving him back something "good" instead.

Above all, keep loving one another earnestly, since love covers a multitude of sins. (1 Peter 4:8)

I Lost My Temper . . .

It'd be wonderful if you never sinned by getting angry ever again, but that's not realistic. At some time you will find yourself responding in sinful anger. So what should you do when you fail?

Repent to God. Tell God that you sinned by getting angry, that you are sorry, and that you want to turn away from sinning like that again. Ask him to forgive you—not only for the sin of anger, but for the sin beneath the sin: whatever you had wanted so badly. (More on this below.)

If we confess our sins, he is faithful and just to forgive us our sins and to cleanse us from all unrighteousness. (1 John 1:9)

Confess to the other person. If you got angry with someone, admit to him that you were wrong; then ask him to forgive you. You probably need to say specifically what you did that was wrong. (Example: "I shouldn't have been angry, yelled at you, and slammed the door.")

Of course, you *shouldn't* confess what you may have been *thinking.* You could really hurt someone if, for example, you were to say, "I've been wrong by wishing

you were dead." Probably not a good idea to share that thought.

Bearing with one another and, if one has a complaint against another, forgiving each other; as the Lord has forgiven you, so you also must forgive. (Colossians 3:13; see also Matthew 5:23–26)

Search your heart.

Ask yourself: "Why was I getting upset? What did I **want** to have or not want to **lose**?" The "thing" your heart desired may be what the Bible calls an "idol." It could be a good thing that you love too much. Confess this "sin beneath the sin" to God and ask him to change what your heart desires.

THINK ABOUT IT

When you are trying to patch things up with someone you've sinned against, here are some things NOT to say . . .

"I'm sorry if I hurt you."
"I'm sorry you were offended."
"I'm sorry, . . . But YOU shouldn't have done . . . ."
"I was kinda wrong."
"They said I had to come tell you I was sorry."
"Mistakes were made."

But it's difficult to improve on this example of what not to say when apologizing. In his *New York Times* article, "The Perfect Non-Apology Apology," Bruce McCall humorously gave this terrifically bad example:

"Nobody is sorrier than me that the police officer had to spend his valuable time writing out a parking ticket on my car. Though from my personal standpoint I know for a certainty that the meter had not yet expired, please accept my expression of deep regret at this unfortunate incident."

8

RULES, RULES, RULES

The first five books of the Bible are often called either the Pentateuch (*penta* means "five") or the Books of the Law. That's because these books contain the laws God gave his people, Israel. He gave these laws to his people to teach them what he's like.

If you count up every single rule in the entire Old Testament, you'll find 248 positive commands: "*Do this!*" And you'll also find 365 negative commands: "*Don't do this!*" That's a total of 613 commands.

So, how could you possibly keep track of all these commands? Maybe you could focus on just a few of the rules. But how would you decide which ones are most important?

Jesus gives the answer. In Mark 12, an expert in the Old Testament laws asked Jesus which rule was the most important one in the Bible. Jesus answered:

"The most important is, 'Hear, O Israel: The Lord our God, the Lord is one. And you shall love the Lord your God with all your heart and with all your soul and with all your mind

248 DOS
+
365 DON'TS
=
613

and with all your strength.' The second is this: 'You shall love your neighbor as yourself.' There is no other commandment greater than these." (Mark 12:29–31)

There it is. You can squeeze all the other commands into just two: love God and love people (Matthew 22:37–40; Romans 13:9). If you truly love God and people, you'll be obeying the rest of the Bible. And if you truly obey the entire Bible, you'll be living out true love for God and people.

● ● ●

THE GOAL OF THIS COMMAND IS LOVE, WHICH COMES FROM A PURE HEART AND A GOOD CONSCIENCE AND A SINCERE FAITH.
1 TIMOTHY 1:5 NIV

● ● ●

But what does loving God and loving people look like in everyday life?

In Luke 10, Jesus discussed these two most important commands (love God and love people). He explained what they mean and then illustrated what it looks like to "love people" by telling the story of the Good Samaritan. You can read it for yourself in Luke 10:29–37. In this story, you'll find that loving people means giving yourself to meet the needs of people around you.

But Luke 10 doesn't end there. After describing what it means to love people, the very next story paints a picture of what it means to love *God*.

When you read this story in Luke 10:38–42, you'll find that a woman named Martha has a problem. She's working busily in the kitchen, giving herself to meet the needs of people around her. She looks, in fact, a lot like a "Good Samaritan." She is trying to love people! So what's the problem?

Martha's sister, Mary, isn't helping her. Instead, she's listening to Jesus. Martha wants Mary's help. But Martha has forgotten about the *most* important command: to love Jesus. Mary remembers it, and so, instead of helping her sister and serving the guests, she sits focused on Jesus's teaching. She loves Jesus even more than she loves her sister.

So loving God means being devoted to Jesus with all your heart and all your life. That's the most important command, and the second is to love people sacrificially.

But can anyone really obey these two commands? Doesn't everybody just naturally want to love herself (Ephesians 5:29)? You can find the key to loving God and others in 1 John 4:19.

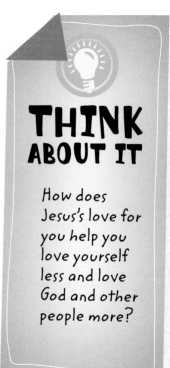

THINK ABOUT IT

How does Jesus's love for you help you love yourself less and love God and other people more?

What command is given most in the Bible? (Answer: "Do not be afraid" [365 times])

31

9

HOW TO CLEAN YOUR ROOM

1. Bed made. Every layer smooth; only the top layer showing.

When I was a kid, my room was always a wreck. Clothes draped over everything, the lost TV remote buried under the bed, shoes and toys all across the floor. You could barely see the carpet.

Then one night something happened. My dad came home from work to find nobody home. The rest of the family was out running an errand and had left the door unlocked. My dad opened the door to my room, saw the huge mess, and immediately reached behind the door to grab my baseball bat. He thought, *Someone has broken into our house! We've been robbed!*

About that time, we pulled back into the driveway, and I had some big explaining to do. Of course, we *hadn't* been robbed. So it didn't take long for my dad to come up with a list telling me what a clean room looks like.

It's been about 30 years since I came home and met my dad with a baseball bat in his hand and steam coming out of his ears. But thanks to him, I'll never forget that night (and I'll never forget this list).

Who had the longest bed in the Bible?

(Answer: Og, king of Bashan had an iron bed 13 feet long and 6 feet wide [Deuteronomy 3:11].)

2. Everything has a place, and everything in its place. Everything that belongs in the room should be arranged by kind in a specific place (books together with other books, toys together with other toys, etc.). **Note:** Stacking should be limited to items that are neatest when they are stacked.

3. Nothing on the floor except furniture, musical instrument, sports gear, shoes (neatly arranged in pairs) or other preapproved items (a plant, a lamp, etc.). Other than these objects, there should be nothing on the floor.

6. Nothing in my room that belongs in another room. Nothing that belongs somewhere else should be left in my room beyond the time it is being used (an empty drinking glass, tools from the garage, bicycle, etc.).

4. Clothes are only allowed to be in four locations: sitting in the dirty clothes hamper, hanging in the closet, folded in the dresser, or laid out and ready to be worn the next day.

5. Trash can emptied and clean. Small trash containers are to be emptied into the medium-sized one in the kitchen or into the big cans outside.

10

HOW WE KNOW THE BIBLE IS TRUE

Best selling author, Plato.

Bible Manuscripts

Plato lived in Greece about 425 years before Jesus. He studied under the legendary teacher Socrates and later taught another world-famous teacher: Aristotle. Plato also started the first university (the Academy of Athens), was great in math and philosophy, and his books basically changed the way people have thought ever since. One smart guy.

We still have ancient copies of Plato's writings in a collection called the *Tetralogies*, which means the "Four Teachings." (*Tetra* means four in Greek.) The oldest copy or "manuscript" of this book was copied by hand in A.D. 895. That's about 1,250 years after Plato wrote it and 1,164 years before photocopiers were invented. Although the *Tetralogies* was a "best-seller" in Plato's time, only 210 ancient hand-written copies still exist.

That's way better than the ancient historian Herodotus. We've got 109 copies of his *Histories*, and only 96 copies of

Thucydides' *History of the Peloponnesian War*. Yet even the book with the most ancient copies—Homer's *Iliad*, with just over 1,800—doesn't compare with the New Testament.

Check out the chart. You don't have to do the math to see that the New Testament has *thousands* of manuscripts! The chart features only three kinds of manuscripts, but if you tried to count *every kind* of manuscript, you'd be busy for a long, long time. Experts say there are over 24,300 manuscripts of the New Testament—with more still being discovered! Such a massive collection of manuscripts shows that for thousands of years God has been protecting his Word. (Turn the page to discover the totals for this chart.)

(Turn the page to discover the totals for this chart.)

✏ ✏ ✏

Look up Psalm 12:6–7. In this passage, God pledges to do something to the Scripture. He has promised to preserve his Word. The huge number of manuscripts reveals that God has indeed kept his word.

century	papyri	uncials	minuscules
2nd	4	-	-
2nd/3rd	2	-	-
3rd	45	2	-
3rd/4th	13	2	-
4th	18	16	-
4th/5th	8	9	-
5th	5	42	-
5th/6th	3	11	-
6th	12	54	-
6th/7th	8	5	-
7th	8	30	-
7th/8th	1	6	-
8th	2	25	-
8th/9th	-	3	-
9th	-	58	14
9th/10th	-	2	4
10th	-	17	140
10th/11th	-	11	18
11th	-	2	425
11th/12th	-	1	42
12th	-	-	549
12th/13th	-	-	41
13th	-	-	563
13th/14th	-	-	40
14th	-	-	522
14th/15th	-	-	8
15th	-	-	240
15th/16th	-	-	5
16th	-	-	148
16th/17th	-	-	1
17th	-	-	48
17th/18th	-	-	-
18th	-	-	17

Who is the oldest person in the Bible?

Methuselah: 969 years (Genesis 5:27)

These thousands of manuscripts also allow us to know exactly what God's Word says. If you compare all these manuscripts, they match up with almost 100 percent precision. From manuscript to manuscript, the wording is almost exactly the same.

If that doesn't sound impressive, try it yourself. Get a blank sheet of paper and copy a page from this book in your own handwriting. Then have someone else carefully compare your copy with the original page from the book. There's a good chance that somewhere you'll have skipped a word or a line.

But in the Bible, and through thousands of manuscripts, God has preserved his Word for his people with incredible accuracy.

*   *   *

The next page features the oldest New Testament manuscript. It was copied down around A.D. 125—less than 30 years after the apostle John wrote the original! It's called P^{52} (the "P" stands for *papyri*; "52" is the number of the manuscript). It contains part of the Gospel according to John, chapter 18. You can still see this manuscript in person at the University of Manchester Library in England.

Did You KNOW?

There are three kinds of Greek manuscripts:

1. Papyri (pronounced puh-pie-ree, named for the special paper it was written on)

2. Uncials (pronounced un-see-uhls, which used only capital letters)

3. Minuscules (pronounced min-uh-skew-uhls, because they only used very tiny, lower case letters)

How many Greek manuscripts are there for the New Testament?

Answer: Papyri = 129; Uncials = 296; Minuscules = 2825; Grand total = 3250

From John 18:31–33

(red letters show the words on the manuscript)

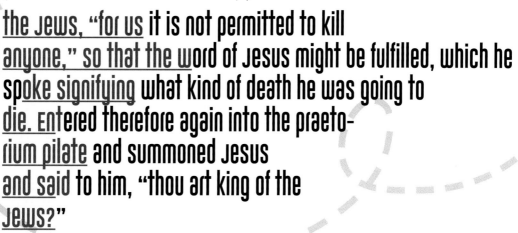

the <u>Jews,</u> "<u>for us</u> it is not permitted to kill
<u>anyone,</u>" <u>so that the w</u>ord of Jesus might be fulfilled, which he
sp<u>oke signifying</u> what kind of death he was going to
<u>die. En</u>tered therefore again into the praeto-
<u>rium pilate</u> and summoned Jesus
<u>and said</u> to him, "thou art king of the
<u>Jews?</u>"

From John 18:37–38

(red letters show the words on the manuscript)

a king I am. For <u>this I have been born</u>
and (for this) I have come into the <u>world so that I would</u>
testify to the truth. Everyone who is <u>of the truth</u>
hears of me my voice." <u>said to him</u>
pilate, "what is truth?" <u>And this</u>
having said, again he went out unto <u>the Jews</u>
and said to them, "I find <u>not one</u>
fault in him."

HOW TO READ STORIES IN THE BIBLE

Heroes are cool. Who doesn't enjoy the Avengers or Batman, Spiderman or Black Widow? They have awesome costumes, sweet vehicles, secret identities, hidden bases, and amazing abilities. Yet most of them are also flawed people with broken pasts who have risen to face those challenges for the good of others. What's not to like?

But when you stop to think about *why* you like heroes, the answer is clear: God made you that way. He created you to appreciate and imitate someone greater than yourself. We're all wired for worship. There's just something that draws us to admire people who have power, looks, money, and influence. And when you go to the Bible, its pages are filled with incredible characters.

When you read the Bible, don't simply try to act like the people in the stories. God isn't telling us about a bunch of heroes who always come through to save the day. Instead, he's showing

how *he* is The Hero, who rescues people who do both good and bad things.

For example, when you read about David and Goliath, remember that David (the boy who would be king one day) fights on behalf of the entire army of Israelites who are too scared to go into battle (1 Samuel 17). Yet this story is written not so you could imitate David the king, but so that you would learn to trust a king who would fight for you. And so it happened that years later another King (Jesus) would wage war in the place of God's people, against their greatest enemies: sin, Satan, and death. Whether in David's day or the time of Jesus, God has always sent a Deliverer to rescue his weak and sinful people. And this Deliverer (not David) is the real Hero.

What about the story of Jonah? Is this famous story about a disobedient prophet? Is it about a huge fish? Or is it about the merciful God who gives second (and third and fourth) chances to people like Jonah, like the Ninevites, and like you and me? Who's the Hero here?

Then what about that story of Mary and Martha? Is Mary the good example and Martha the bad example? Who's the hero here? In this story, Jesus gently calls Martha's attention to how she is more interested in getting her work done than in listening to his teaching. As you read, looking for the real

Hero, you'll see that this story is more about "gracious Jesus" than "good Mary" or "distracted Martha."

🍃 🍃 🍃

YOU SEARCH THE SCRIPTURES BECAUSE YOU THINK THEY GIVE YOU ETERNAL LIFE. BUT THE SCRIPTURES POINT TO ME! JOHN 5:39 NLT

🍃 🍃 🍃

And what do you see in the story of the feeding of the crowd of 5,000 people (John 6)? Is it more a lesson in sharing or an amazing example of what Jesus can do with the little you give him?

When you read the stories of the Bible, take notice of the men and women. You'll see good examples and bad examples. But most of all—be on the lookout for the greatest Hero of all: God himself!

12

HOW TO MAKE YOUR OWN SLING

The book of 1 Samuel, chapter 17, tells how God used a boy (David) to defeat a giant (Goliath). David didn't use a gun (they weren't invented yet). David didn't use a spear or bow and arrow. No, this shepherd boy used something called a sling.

David's sling was most likely a small leather pouch with a strap tied to each end. It was used one-handed. One strap would be wrapped around one finger, while the other strap was held between the thumb and first finger. The object to be thrown would then be placed inside the pouch.

Then the pouch would be twirled faster and faster in a wide circle above the head. Once the sling was circling at full speed, the one strap being held between thumb and first finger would be released, sending the object sailing through the air.

If you want to get a feel for how the sling worked, here's a toy version you can make and practice throwing up into the air and catching.

Objects you will need: a large rubber band; a tennis ball (or even better, a soft lacrosse practice ball); and a lightweight, long sock or, better yet, one of those long skinny plastic bags that newspapers come in.

1. Put the ball inside the sock or plastic bag, all the way to the end.

2. While holding the ball tightly against the end of the sock, wrap the rubber band around the sock. This should keep the ball from moving around.

3. Hold the sock by the tail—the end furthest from the ball. Twirl the sock around your head, then release the tail to send the whole thing flying.

It'll take some time to become an expert with this sling, but you can use it in many ways. Throw it overhand or underhand; play catch with a friend; or just see how far or high you can throw it. You can also use it instead of a Frisbee to play a modified version of Ultimate Frisbee.

REMEMBER: Be safe when using your sling! You should never use the sling to throw a ball or other object at another person and should always be aware of what is around you before using the sling.

13

WHAT EVERY KID NEEDS

J. C. Ryle was born in England in 1816. Growing up he loved sports and school. When he was in college at Oxford, he was on the rowing and cricket teams. (Cricket is kind of like baseball, except even harder to really understand.) Ryle became a Christian at the age of 22 and a pastor a few years later.

For the next 62 years, Ryle served as pastor, author, and church leader until a year before his death at the age of 84. One of his books, *Thoughts for Young Men*, is over 100 years old! Yet it still offers great advice for both boys and girls who want to follow Jesus. Here's just a taste of what Ryle said:

1. "Try to get a clear view of sin."

Nothing has caused more misery, sadness, and pain in the world than sin. The Bible teaches that sin has not only messed up the world *around* us, it has also changed *us*. We don't come into this world neutral; we're born with a nature that wants to rebel against God. Yet God sent Jesus to take the punishment our rebellion deserves. This shows just how bad our sins really are: they cost the life of Jesus Christ to pay for them. Sin is awful.

2. "Seek to become personally acquainted with our Lord Jesus Christ."

Since Jesus gave up his own life to die for sinners, God the Father has honored him. He has been exalted to the Father's throne and is the Ruler of this world. The entire Bible is all about him—the Old Testament anticipates him, the New Testament announces him. He is the foundation of our faith, the Source of everything we really need, and the One we should always turn to for help.

3. "Never forget that nothing is so important as your soul."

Humans are not just very advanced animals. Unlike the other creatures God made, human beings will live somewhere forever. And your life here on planet earth is like the rehearsal for eternity. Every soul must answer this one essential question: Where are you taking refuge to escape from the penalty of your sin? Those who turn to Christ Jesus as their Refuge and Rescuer, will find forgiveness and eternal protection and joy in his presence.

4. "It is possible for even a young person to serve God."

You don't have to wait until you're grown up to be serious about God. Think about it: you've known that

THINK ABOUT IT

"He is no fool who gives up what he cannot keep to gain that which he cannot lose."

—Jim Elliot, missionary martyr

certain things were wrong (or right) since you were very little. You are responsible to God for your words, actions, and attitudes. Following Jesus is not an easy path, but it's the best path. Ask Jesus to help you trust and obey him. He will give you faith, and you will learn how to live as one of his followers. You won't regret it.

5. As long as you live, make the Bible your strength and guide.

For the Christian, God's Word is a fountain of spiritual life and nourishment. As you read the Bible, ask God (the Holy Spirit) to teach you. Take time to read the Bible regularly. God's Word is daily food, but it's also a light that shows you the way to go.

MORE TO EXPLORE ▶ If you'd like to learn more of what J. C. Ryle has to say, you may want to read his book *Thoughts for Young Men.*

14

FAMOUS BIBLE PHRASES (& FAKES!)

Recently, two thousand Americans were asked questions about the Bible. Out of the whole group, about 1,760 (88%) said they owned a Bible, yet only 380 people (19%) read it regularly (at least four times per week).

This means that while many people may say, "Sure, I know the Bible," the fact is most of them don't know much about it.

It's no surprise then that many people might not even realize when they're quoting the Bible in their conversations. And at other times, people may think they are quoting God's Word, but they actually aren't.

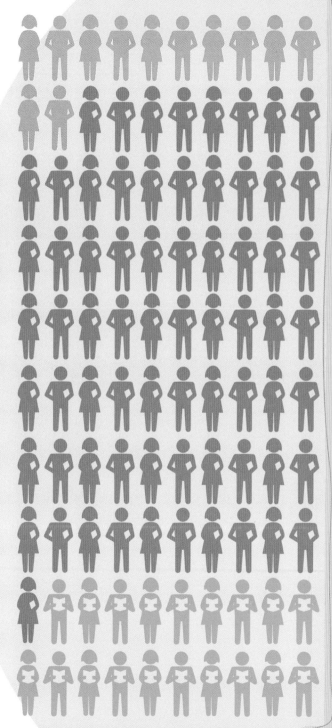

88%
OWN A BIBLE

ONLY
19%
READ THE BIBLE

BIBLE PHRASES

Bible Phrases

If you know your Bible well, you'll recognize these phrases, which are often used in everyday conversations. All thirty come right out of the Bible.

"A DROP IN THE BUCKET" Isaiah 40:15

"A FLY IN THE OINTMENT" Ecclesiastes 10:1

"A GOOD SAMARITAN" Luke 10:30-37

"A LABOR OF LOVE" 1 Thessalonians 1:3

"AM I MY BROTHER'S KEEPER?" Genesis 4:9

"AN EYE FOR AN EYE" Exodus 21:24 & Matthew 5:38

"AT THEIR WIT'S END" Psalm 107:27

"CAST THE FIRST STONE." John 8:7

"DON'T CAST YOUR PEARLS BEFORE SWINE." Matthew 7:6

"GO THE EXTRA MILE." Matthew 5:41

"EAT, DRINK, AND BE MERRY." Luke 12:19

"BY THE SKIN OF YOUR TEETH" Job 19:20

"HE WHO LIVES BY THE SWORD, DIES BY THE SWORD." Matthew 26:52

"IT'S BETTER TO GIVE THAN TO RECEIVE." Acts 20:35

"NOTHING BUT SKIN AND BONES" Job 19:19-20

"PRIDE COMES BEFORE A FALL." Proverbs 16:18

"SEE EYE TO EYE" Isaiah 52:8

"SET YOUR TEETH ON EDGE" Jeremiah 31:30

"THE APPLE OF HIS EYE" Psalm 17:8

"THE BLIND LEADING THE BLIND" Matthew 15:13-14

"THE SALT OF THE EARTH" Matthew 5:13

"THE STRAIGHT AND NARROW" Matthew 7:14

"THE TWINKLING OF AN EYE" 1 Corinthians 15:52

"THE WISDOM OF SOLOMON" Luke 11:31

"THE WRITING ON THE WALL" Daniel 5:5

"THERE'S NOTHING NEW UNDER THE SUN." Ecclesiastes 1:9

"TO EVERYTHING THERE IS A SEASON." Ecclesiastes 3:1

"WHAT GOD HAS JOINED TOGETHER, LET NO MAN PUT ASUNDER." Matthew 19:6

"WOLVES IN SHEEP'S CLOTHING" Matthew 7:15

"YOU REAP WHAT YOU SOW." Galatians 6:7

BIBLE FAKES

Bible Fakes
You'd search God's Word a long time before finding any of the expressions listed on this page.

"GOD HELPS THOSE WHO HELP THEMSELVES."

This is not in the Bible; it's probably from ancient storyteller, Aesop. Thankfully, God helps *needy* people who call on him, not strong people who are able to help themselves.

"MONEY IS THE ROOT OF ALL EVIL."

First Timothy 6:10 says that "the *love* of money is the root of all kinds of evil," not that money itself is the source of all evil.

"A PENNY SAVED IS A PENNY EARNED."

This saying may be something penned by Benjamin Franklin.

"TO THINE OWN SELF BE TRUE."

This expression comes from William Shakespeare's play, *Hamlet*.

"THIS TOO SHALL PASS."

It is true that one day God will make everything new in the new heavens and new earth. But this quote is not from the Bible.

"SPARE THE ROD AND SPOIL THE CHILD."

The Bible teaches that parents should discipline their children. But this particular saying does not come from Scripture.

"CLEANLINESS IS NEXT TO GODLINESS."

It's not that God wants you to stay dirty and smelly, but—happily for some kids—this verse is not in the Bible.

15

HOW TO READ THE BIBLE EVERY DAY

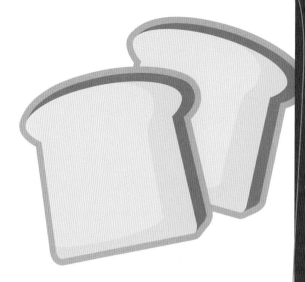

A round the year 1452, German printer, Johannes Gutenberg, printed the first Bible using movable-type printing. For the first time, Bibles didn't have to be copied by hand. This new kind of printing press eventually led to Bibles being printed and sold cheaply enough for regular people to buy them. Spiritual food for hungry souls.

Today the Bible has been translated into over 2,500 languages. Many translations of the Bible are available for English speakers. Just like eating food enables us to live and grow physically, reading the Bible gives us food to grow spiritually.

But how do you go about making Bible reading a regular part of your life? **What's most important is not how much Bible you read everyday, but how well you are being fed by God's Word. It's great to try to master the Bible. It's even better to let the Bible master you.**

"MAN SHALL NOT LIVE BY BREAD ALONE, BUT BY EVERY WORD THAT COMES FROM THE MOUTH OF GOD."
MATTHEW 4:4

HERE ARE SOME TIPS TO GET STARTED:

1. **Get a good translation.** If you don't have a Bible, here are several translations (or "versions") that will serve your Bible reading well:

- *The English Standard Version* (ESV)—many consider this the best all-around translation.
- *The New International Version* (NIV)—highly readable, easy for reading long sections.
- *The New American Standard Bible* (NASB)—excellent for careful studying of Scripture.
- *The New Living Translation* (NLT)—easiest to read.

2. **Have a plan.** Many Christians set a New Year's resolution that over the next year they will read the entire Bible. This is a great goal, although the Bible never says you have to read its sixty-six books within twelve months. However, if you're up to the challenge, here are some ways to read the Bible in one year (or three years).

The Bible contains 1,189 chapters. So if you read about three chapters a day (3.25753424657534 chapters, to be exact), then you'll be done in 365 days. (Or if you read one chapter a day, you can finish in about three years.) If you're looking for

EAT THIS BOOK

When we eat food, we taste it, chew it, enjoy (savor) it, and digest it. It's the same way with God's Word. Here are some Latin words that describe how to "eat" Scripture:

LECTIO ("read" the Word)—like tasting food

MEDITATIO ("meditate" on the Word)—like chewing food

ORATIO ("pray" the Word)—like savoring food

CONTEMPLATIO ("contemplate" the Word)—like digesting food

a good place in the Bible to start, you may want to try Mark's Gospel or Psalms or Proverbs. You may also want to check out the *YouVersion* app or the *glo Bible* app for helpful ways to read God's Word on your tablet or phone.

3. Find a place and time. Find a quiet spot in your house and in your day to focus on God's Word. Perhaps it's your bedroom before breakfast. Or maybe it's at the kitchen table at some other time. You may find it helpful to turn off the TV and other electronic devices (unless, of course, you're using an app for your Bible reading). Find something that works for you, and stick with it.

4. Ask God to help you. The Bible is your spiritual food, but only God can help you digest what you've eaten. Sometimes reading the Bible may seem boring; but if *God* helps you study, it can be breathtaking. This is why God gave us the prayer in Psalm 119:18: "Open my eyes, that I may behold wondrous things [things that fill me with wonder and awe] out of your law."

5. Read S-L-O-W-L-Y. Take your time and use your mind to "chew" on God's Word. Look at the passage carefully. When you read too fast, as super-detective Sherlock Holmes said, "You see, but you do not *observe*." So slow down by asking questions about what you are reading: *Why does it say that? What does that mean? How do you do that?* Don't wolf down Scripture. Savor each bite.

6. Look for God. The Bible's main purpose is not to be your handy guidebook for life. It's not mainly a rule book, science book, history book, or storybook. It was written to reveal God—what he is like, what he's done, and how incredible he is. It's natural that you won't understand everything in the Bible. So when you read, don't get so tangled up by something confusing that you forget about God! Try to learn something each day about *him*.

7. Write down your thoughts. When you finish reading and thinking, you might want to take a few minutes to record what God taught you. You could use a 3 x 5 card, notepad, or computer tablet to jot down a few sentences about what you've learned. You could simply make a list of what God is like—a short "biography of God" for the day. Many people will write down what they've learned in the form of a prayer, addressed to the Lord.

8. Think about what you learned. The best thoughts are worth reviewing later in the day. Re-read your notes and ask the Lord to help you understand and trust it even more than before. The Bible calls this kind of thinking: "meditation." It's like scriptural snacking. *Bon appétit!*

Bon appétit!

16

LEARN THE HEBREW ALPHABET

What language did Moses use to write the first books of the Old Testament? What language did King David use to write Psalms?

רֵאשִׁית
(ray-SHEETH)
BEGINNING

בָּרָא
(bah-RAH)
CREATE

אֱלֹהִים
(eh-lo-HEEM)
GOD

The answer is Hebrew. To people who speak English, Hebrew is read "backwards," from the right side of the page to the left. In English, of course, you read left to right. (?naem I tahw wonk uoy oD)

Almost the entire Old Testament is written in ancient Hebrew. Only Daniel 2:4—7:28; Ezra 4:8—6:18 and 7:12–26; Jeremiah 10:11; and two words in Genesis 31:47 are not in Hebrew. They are written in a similar language called Aramaic.

Originally, the Hebrew alphabet contained 23 consonants and no vowels! People who spoke Hebrew automatically knew which vowels were supposed to go with which words. Do you think that's even possible? Tht knd f thng cld nvr wrk! Tht wld b rlly, rlly dffclt, dn't y thnk?

Hebrew doesn't have an upper case or lower case. For example, the first letter of a sentence or a name is the same size and

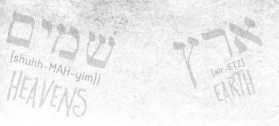

שָׁמַיִם
(shuhh-MAH-yim))
HEAVENS

אֶרֶץ
(air-ETZ)
EARTH

shape as the rest of the letters.

The Hebrew used in the Bible is different from modern-day Hebrew. It is known as a "dead" language. No one today speaks this language or knows exactly what it sounded like.

Now try this: look closely at this series of Hebrew characters and pick out the Hebrew words written at the top of the page. (Hint: see Genesis 1:1.)

בְּרֵאשִׁית בָּרָא אֱלֹהִם אֵת הַשָּׁמַיִם וְאֵת הָאָרֶץ

LETTER	NAME	ENGLISH EQUIVALENT
א	aleph (AHH-leff)	No equivalent in English, a silent letter.
ב	beyth (BAY-th)	B as in Boba Fett
ג	gimel (GIMM-ull)	G as in Greedo
ד	daleth (DAHL-eth)	D as in Darth Vader
ה	hey (HAY)	H as in Han Solo
ו	waw (WOW)	W as in Watto
ז	zayin (ZAHH-yunn)	Z as in Ziro
ח	cheyth (KHAY-th)	Kh as in Khetanna
ט	teyth (TAY-th)	T as in Tarkin
י	yod (YOE-dth)	Y as in Yoda
כ or ך	kaph (KAFF)	K as in Kylo Ren
ל	lamed (LAHM-edd)	L as in Luke
מ or ם	meym (MAME)	M as in Maul
נ or ן	nun (NOON)	N as in Naboo
ס	samek (SAMM-eck)	S as in Saber
ע	'ayin (EYE-yun)	No equivalent in English, a silent letter.
פ	pay (PAY)	P as in Palpatine
צ or ץ	tsadey (TSAH-dee)	Tz as in TZ-33
ק	qoph (KOAF)	Q as in Qui-Gon
ר	reysh (RAY-sh)	R as in Rey
שׂ	sin (SEEN)	S as in Sarco Plank
שׁ	shin (SHEEN)	Sh as in shuttle
ת	taw (TOW, like cow)	T as in Tatooine

17

SIXTY-SIX IN ONE

You may know a person named Mark or Ruth, but do you know what their Bible book is about? Here's a quick description of all 66 books of the Bible.

THE OLD TESTAMENT

HISTORY (& LAW)

Genesis—The story of how God made the world, how people sinned, and how God began to fix it.

Exodus—The story of how God delivered his people from slavery in Egypt.

Leviticus—The laws God gave his people to tell them the right way to live.

Numbers—More laws from God and stories about how God's people failed to obey them.

Deuteronomy—Moses retells the story of God's love and mercy to his people.

Joshua—The story of how God gave his people the land he had promised them.

Judges—The story of how God raised up leaders to rescue his sinful people again and again.

Ruth—The story of how God loved Ruth and made her a part of his people and a part of his plan for a Savior.

1–2 Samuel—The story of the prophet Samuel and how God spoke through him to his people Israel.

1–2 Kings—The history of Israel's good kings and bad kings.

1–2 Chronicles—A retellng of the story of how God loved his people, even as their leaders failed them.

Ezra–Nehemiah—The story of how God brought his people back into the land he had given them.

Esther—The story of how God protected his people when they were prisoners in Babylon.

POETRY & WISDOM

Job—The story of how a man learned to trust God through terrible trials and suffering.

Psalms—A collection of worship songs written by King David and others.

Proverbs—Wise sayings that King Solomon and others wrote and collected.

Ecclesiastes— A book that teaches how life without God is meaningless.

Song of Solomon—A beautiful love song between a husband and wife.

MAJOR PROPHETS ("MAJOR" BECAUSE THEY'RE LONGER)

Isaiah—A warning to God's people to turn from their sin with a promise God would send a deliverer.

Jeremiah—A collection of sermons warning God's people that they will be kicked out of their land because of their rebellion, and one day, brought back.

Lamentations—A collection of laments ("sad songs") mourning the sin of God's people and the discipline they have experienced from God.

Ezekiel—A collection of sermons and visions that warn and encourage God's sinful people after they had been kicked out of their land.

Daniel—A collection of stories meant to teach us how God protects his people from their enemies.

MINOR PROPHETS ("MINOR" BECAUSE THEY'RE SHORTER)

Hosea—A collection of stories meant to teach us how God loves his sinful people.

Joel—A sermon warning of God's coming judgment and promising an outpouring of his Spirit.

Amos—A collection of sermons about God's judgment on all who sin, and a call to love and care for the poor.

Obadiah—A sermon against people who proudly resist God and his people.

Jonah—The story of how God loves to rescue sinful people.

Micah—A warning against people who cling to sin and a promise of forgiveness to people who turn from their sin.

Nahum—A collection of sermons against sinful and proud people.

Habakkuk—A sermon encouraging people to trust God even when evil seems to be winning.

Zephaniah—A collection of sermons about the future when God will judge wicked people and rescue his own people.

Haggai—A collection of sermons about how God will one day come to live with his people again.

Zechariah—Sermons encouraging God's people that he has a future plan for all who are faithful to him.

Malachi—Sermons that accuse God's people of being half-hearted in their love for him.

TURN THE PAGE FOR: THE NEW TESTAMENT

THE NEW TESTAMENT

GOSPELS

Matthew—The eyewitness story of Jesus who came as the promised King from King David's line.

Mark—The fast-paced story of Jesus and how he came to save us from our sin.

Luke—A detailed account of how Jesus reached out to the undeserving and gave his life for them.

John— The eyewitness account of Jesus's ministry on earth and how he taught us about his Father.

HISTORY

Book of Acts—The story of how the good news about Jesus spread through the known world.

PAUL'S EPISTLES ("LETTERS") TO CHURCHES

Romans—A letter explaining just how sinful we are and how God provided a Savior.

1 Corinthians—A letter written to help a church with a ton of problems learn how to trust and love Jesus.

2 Corinthians—A letter that reminds Christians that God chooses weak people and shows his strength through them.

Galatians—A letter that explains and defends the gospel against those who would want to add "works" to our salvation.

Ephesians—A letter that tells the amazing story of how God chooses and redeems his people and will one day restore and unite all things in Jesus.

Philippians—A letter encouraging Christians to let the good news about Jesus make them joyful even through hard times.

Colossians—A letter teaching Christians to let their thoughts and lives be shaped by the good news about Jesus.

1 Thessalonians—A letter encouraging Christians to keep growing in their walk with Jesus even when it's hard.

2 Thessalonians—A letter reminding Christians to live faithful lives until Jesus returns.

PAUL'S EPISTLES ("LETTERS") TO INDIVIDUALS

1 Timothy—A letter encouraging Timothy to be strong and lead his church in light of the good news about Jesus.

2 Timothy—A letter reminding Timothy to guard the good news about Jesus.

Titus—A letter that warns against false teachers.

Philemon—A letter asking one Christian to forgive another Christian.

GENERAL EPISTLES ("LETTERS")

Hebrews—A sermon that explains how the Old Testament points to Jesus.

James—A letter encouraging Christians to express their faith by loving others in practical ways.

1 Peter—A letter encouraging suffering Christians to live holy lives.

2 Peter—A letter warning against false teachers.

1 John—A letter about how God first loves us through Jesus and fills us with his love for others and for his truth.

2 John—A letter warning against false teachers.

3 John—A letter encouraging Christians to welcome others, especially missionaries.

Jude—A letter warning the church against false teachers.

APOCALYPTIC WRITING

Revelation—Visions from God that show how Jesus will one day return and win the battle over sin, Satan, suffering, and death.

18

HAPPY HOLIDAYS

If you've read the Old Testament, you've probably encountered some of the 613 rules that God gave his people. But it may surprise you that some of the commands sounded something like *"Let's have a party!"*

God didn't want his people merely to do his bidding—like robots. He also wanted them to enjoy him—like family. So God set up festivals or "feast days" to give his people a break: a time to reflect on all he had done for them. These were happy and holy-days. (It's easy to see how our word "holiday" comes from the idea of a "holy day.")

The wheel diagram shows the important days and seasons of

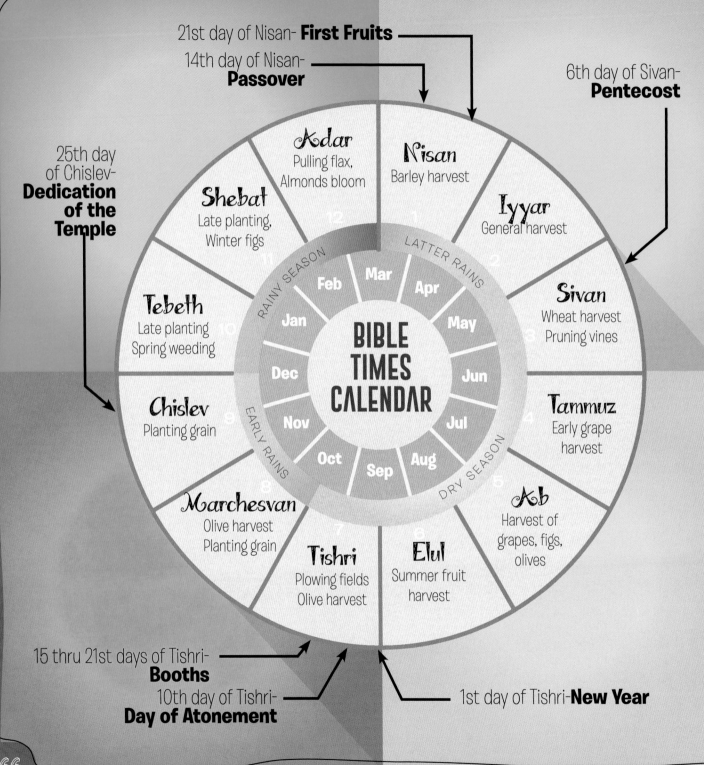

21st day of Nisan- **First Fruits**

14th day of Nisan- **Passover**

6th day of Sivan- **Pentecost**

25th day of Chislev- **Dedication of the Temple**

Adar
Pulling flax, Almonds bloom
12

Nisan
Barley harvest
1

Iyyar
General harvest
2

Shebat
Late planting, Winter figs
11

Sivan
Wheat harvest Pruning vines
3

Tebeth
Late planting Spring weeding
10

Tammuz
Early grape harvest
4

Chislev
Planting grain
9

Ab
Harvest of grapes, figs, olives
5

Marchesvan
Olive harvest Planting grain
8

Tishri
Plowing fields Olive harvest
7

Elul
Summer fruit harvest
6

RAINY SEASON

LATTER RAINS

EARLY RAINS

DRY SEASON

Feb Mar Apr
Jan May
Dec Jun
Nov Jul
Oct Aug
Sep

BIBLE TIMES CALENDAR

15 thru 21st days of Tishri- **Booths**

10th day of Tishri- **Day of Atonement**

1st day of Tishri- **New Year**

66

the calendar used by God's people in Bible times. Use the diagram to answer the following questions:

What was farm life like around the time of the Passover?

How many more months did it take wheat to grow, as compared to barley?

What produce items would most likely have still been on the menu in January?

What would have been your favorite month of the year? Why?

In what Jewish month is your birthday located?

Major Hebrew Holidays

In Bible times, every Jewish man was required to travel to the capital city of Jerusalem for three feasts each year: Passover, Pentecost, and the Feast of Booths. But the most holy day of the year wasn't a feast; it was a fast: the Day of Atonement.

Day of Atonement

The Day of Atonement was so serious that everyone "fasted"—stopped eating—in preparation for it (Leviticus 16:1). On this Day, the high priest sacrificed a bull for his and his family's sin before sacrificing a goat for the sins of God's people. The Day of Atonement showed both the holiness of

God and the mercy of God. All people, even the best people, need to have their sin forgiven.

Jesus, the ultimate high priest, "entered once for all into the holy places, not by means of the blood of goats and calves but by means of his own blood, thus securing an eternal redemption" (Hebrews 9:12).

Feast of Booths

Five days after the Day of Atonement, God wanted his people to celebrate for seven days (Exodus 23:16,17; 34:22). During these days, the Israelites camped out in huts made from tree branches (Leviticus 23:33–44). The Feast of Booths was a time to recall how God had taken care of his people for the forty years they had lived in tents in the wilderness (Leviticus 23:43). Eventually this celebration included a water-pouring ceremony, which pictured how God had provided water for his people in the wilderness.

In John's Gospel, Jesus stands up on the seventh day of the Feast of Booths and announces that God has again provided life-giving water for his people. He says,

"If anyone thirsts, let him come to me and drink. Whoever believes in me, as the Scripture has said, 'Out of his heart will flow rivers of living water.' " Now this he said about the Spirit, whom those who believed in him were to receive. John 7:37–39

Passover

The Passover celebrated the time when God rescued his people from Egypt. For this feast, families sacrificed a perfect lamb (Leviticus 23:5) and painted its blood on the top and sides of the doorway to their house (Exodus 12:22). During the week following Passover, Israel celebrated the Feast of Unleavened Bread. This feast reminded them of the kind of bread God's people ate on the night they were delivered from slavery in Egypt.

In the New Testament, Jesus Christ sacrificed his life as the ultimate Passover Lamb (1 Corinthians 5:7). By giving his life, he rescued his people from eternal death.

Pentecost

This feast occurred seven weeks after Passover and celebrated the crops harvested at the end of the barley harvest

(Leviticus 23:15; Deuteronomy 16:16). The focus of this feast was thanking God for generously providing a bountiful harvest. God's people also expressed their thanksgiving by providing for those in need (Deuteronomy 16:9–12).

The New Testament teaches that at Pentecost, fifty days after Jesus's resurrection, God once again provided for his people. He didn't provide just a harvest of grain to gather into barns, but a harvest of men and women gathered into his kingdom by his Holy Spirit (Acts 2:1–11, 41).

In the Old Testament, God commanded his people to offer sacrifices. These sacrifices showed that someone's sin may be transferred to and paid for by someone else: a substitute. Yet none of these sacrifices could really take away sin (Hebrews 10:4, 11). After all, how could a simple animal be a legitimate substitute for a human being? So the Old Testament sacrifices showed that God's people needed a truly human Substitute. We know today that this true Lamb of God is Jesus Christ. Here's a list of the various sacrifices that God commanded in the Old Testament era.

BURNT OFFERING
Dedication—burning the entire animal demonstrated full commitment to God

Jesus's Sacrifice...
Showed his complete dedication to the Father

GRAIN OFFERING
Giving—offering back to God part of what he had provided as tribute honoring to him

Jesus's Sacrifice...
Gave everything, holding nothing back

FELLOWSHIP OFFERING
Fellowship—expressing enjoyment of the relationship with LORD and with his people

Jesus's Sacrifice...
Restored our relationship to the Father

PEACE OFFERING
Forgiveness—substituting an animal in place of the sinner, representing the cleansing of sin

Jesus's Sacrifice...
Brought forgiveness of sin

GUILT OFFERING
Restoration—removal of guilt often included making restitution

Jesus's Sacrifice...
Removed our guilt

19

FAMOUS TRIPS IN THE BIBLE

I f you needed to go somewhere in Old Testament times, let's hope you owned some good sandals. Walking was slow, but the most common way to travel (Joshua 1:3). On foot, a person might cover 20 miles per day. But a shepherd could spend an entire day guiding a flock of sheep just 6 miles. If you didn't want to walk, then donkeys were the next most common way of getting around (Genesis 22:3, 5). Riding a donkey might bring the distance you could travel in a day to about 23 miles.

Camels and horses weren't used much for transportation in Israel until much later. But, if you were rich and in a hurry, your horse-drawn carriage or chariot could cover about 45 miles per day.

Genesis 37 tells about a trip on foot, when Jacob sent his favorite son, Joseph, to find his older brothers. This trip went north, from Hebron (in the southern part of Israel) to Shechem (in central Israel) and covered 53 miles. (Use a printed or online map to find places that are 53 miles from your home. Imagine what you'd have to do to walk this distance?) When Joseph didn't find his brothers in Shechem, he learned they had gone to Dothan—another 13 miles away.

Using the chart on the next page and the average speeds given above, how long would

Did You KNOW ?

The usual distance between the two front tires of today's car is between 56 and 62 inches. In Bible times, chariots, wagons, and carriages were a bit wider: between 59 and 69 inches.

A two-lane main road in ancient Israel stretched about 10–16 feet across, with smaller, one-lane roads just over 8 feet wide. Today the typical two-lane road is about 24 feet wide.

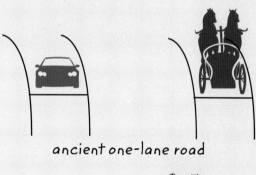

ancient one-lane road

typical two-lane road today

it have taken to make these Bible trips by walking? By chariot? (To get your bearings, you may also want to pinpoint the various cities using the maps at the end of a Bible.)

- Jacob's trip on foot from Bethel to Haran (Genesis 28–29)

- Daniel's trip from Jerusalem to Babylon (Daniel 1:1–3)

- King Josiah and his army's trip from Jerusalem to Carchemish (2 Chronicles 35:20–24)

- Abraham's trip from Ur to Haran (Genesis 11:31–32)

- Abraham's trip from Haran to Shechem (Genesis 12:1–7)

- The trip Jonah should have taken from Joppa to Nineveh (Jonah 1:1–3)

	Babylon	Beersheba	Bethel	Carchemish	Damascus	Haran	Hebron	Jericho	Jerusalem	Joppa	Nineveh	Shechem	Ur
Babylon	0	36	869	479	724	442	901	869	880	868	264	847	170
Beersheba	930	0	58	484	206	549	28	61	47	62	752	78	1100
Bethel	869	58	0	423	145	488	31	12	11	32	691	22	1039
Carchemish	479	484	423	0	278	65	455	423	434	366	285	401	649
Damascus	724	206	145	278	0	343	177	134	149	133	546	123	894
Haran	442	549	488	65	343	0	520	488	500	396	215	466	612
Hebron	901	28	31	455	177	520	0	36	21	45	723	53	1071
Jericho	869	61	12	423	134	488	36	0	15	43	691	26	1039
Jerusalem	880	47	11	434	149	500	21	15	0	36	702	33	1050
Joppa	868	62	32	366	133	396	45	43	36	0	548	36	1038
Nineveh	264	752	691	285	546	215	723	691	702	548	0	669	434
Shechem	847	78	22	401	123	466	53	26	33	36	669	0	1017
Ur	170	1100	1039	649	894	612	1071	1039	1050	1038	434	1017	0

20

FINDING THE CENTER OF THE UNIVERSE

The sun sits at the center of our solar system—92,960,000 miles from earth. When you try to comprehend such an enormous number, it's difficult to grasp the sheer vastness of the empty space between our planet and the sun. Imagine placing a basketball at one end of a basketball court. That represents the sun. Then place a sesame seed or popcorn kernel (something about 0.108 inches in diameter) at the other end of the court, halfway between the foul line and the end of the court. That's the earth!

The sun stands incredibly far away, yet it gives light to the planets and holds them all in orbit. It's also gigantic! If you could fill a huge bucket with everything in our solar system, the sun alone would take up 99 percent of the bucket! Because of this massiveness, everything in our solar system circles in orbit around this flaming, yellow star. It's the center of our solar system.

So, *what's at the center of your life*? What hugely important thing does your life orbit around? Sports? Books? Games? Technology? Your looks? Your friends? Your achievement? Your family? You?

What would be the problem with trying to put something good, like sports or school, at the center of your life? The issue is that whatever you put there—no matter how good or worthwhile—is not designed to fill that central space. It's too

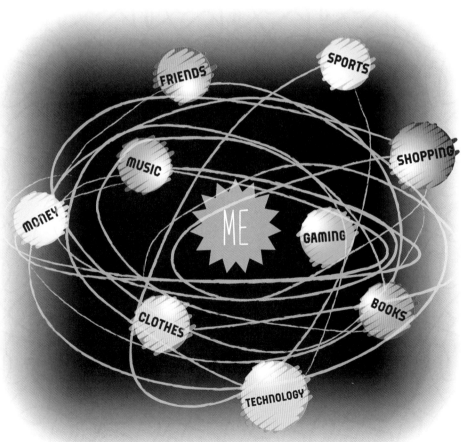

small; there's not enough mass. For example, if you look to friends to be the main thing in your life, at some time they will fail you. God gave you all the good things in your life, but not for them to stand at the center (Psalm 20:7–9).

The Bible says that only God himself is substantial enough to stand at the center of your life. When he is at the center of your universe, all the "planets" are held in the proper place—

you can enjoy friends and sports, school and technology. All these may fail you, but if God is most important, then losing those good things will hurt but won't wreck your life (Habakkuk 3:17–19).

"God at the center of everything" is what the Bible also calls "glorifying God" or "magnifying God." This means that you are recognizing just how massive and massively good God is (Jeremiah 10:6).

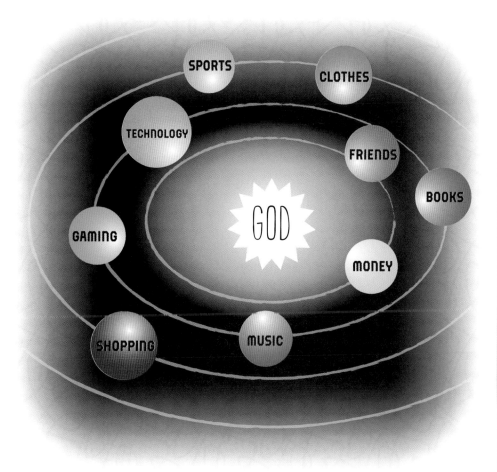

> "GOD IS MOST GLORIFIED IN US WHEN WE ARE MOST SATISFIED IN HIM."
> JOHN PIPER

> "LIFE IS NOT ABOUT YOU. LIFE IS ABOUT GOD AND WHAT HE IS DOING."
> ERIC SIPE

Here's one way to live with God at the center of your universe: when you enjoy something, give God thanks for it. By thanking him, you are acknowledging him as the Source of what you enjoy—God is the one who made competitive sports, or strong legs, or good food, or exciting stories, or great friends. Don't enjoy the warmth that comes from the sun and forget about the Son himself! Feel the warmth every day, and give thanks!

MORE TO EXPLORE If you'd like to learn more about God being your treasure, you may want to read *Thoughts to Make Your Heart Sing* by Sally Lloyd-Jones.

THINK ABOUT IT

BIG UNIVERSE, BIGGER GOD

The Voyager 1 space probe is traveling into outer space at a speed of about 38,500 miles per hour (mph). To put this into perspective, passenger jets fly at around 600 mph. In other words, the speed of the space probe is about 64 times faster than a jet. At "space probe speed," you could travel from New York to Los Angeles in 4 minutes 40 seconds.

At 38,500 mph, it would take only a little over 6 hours for the probe to reach the moon, which is 240,000 miles from earth. And it would take about 52 days to reach the planet Mars. Now if you wanted to visit Saturn, you might want someone to feed your pet for you, because you'd be gone 4 years 9 months. Voyager 1 launched in 1977 and now, after traveling so fast for almost 40 years, it is approaching the outer edge of our solar system.

But let's not stop there. Do you know how long it would take to reach Proxima Centauri, the closest star to our own sun? Even at a blazing 38,500 mph, that trip would take 80,000 years!

Pushing the boundaries of our minds and distances, did you realize that a journey across the Milky Way Galaxy would take 26 billion years? One more crazy number: it is estimated that the universe has 200 billion galaxies. Yikes!

Our God is the God who made all this. But even more mind-blowing is that this same God knows the precise number of hairs on your head (Matthew 10:30). When you think about all this, God wants you to "fear not" (Luke 12:7). This infinitely powerful God is your Father who cares for you his child (Matthew 7:11). In comparison with God and our universe, we humans are pretty tiny. Yet, God sacrificed his beloved Son so that we might enjoy him forever (1 Pet. 3:18).

21

WHAT TO DO WHEN YOU ARE AFRAID

What are you afraid of?

Are you afraid of being all alone in the dark?

Are you afraid of being embarrassed in front of your friends?

How do you feel about big, hairy spiders? (And I'm sure you're only imagining that there's one softly creeping up the back of your neck right now!)

You probably already know that the Bible regularly teaches that you should not be afraid.

What may surprise you is that right alongside commands to "not fear," the Bible also teaches that there is something you *should* fear! What? The answer is God.

Fearing the Lord means being in awe of God, living in the reality that he is God (and you are not). And this "fear of the Lord" will help you not be afraid. Here's how that works. When you're afraid, the things you fear (friends, spiders, dark rooms, etc.) are too big in your mind, and God is too small. Think about what the Bible teaches about being afraid and fearing God:

And do not fear those who kill the body but cannot kill the soul. Rather fear him who can destroy both soul and body in hell. (Matthew 10:28)

When I am afraid, I put my trust in you. (Psalm 56:3)

Fear not, for I am with you; be not dismayed, for I am your God; I will strengthen you, I will help you, I will uphold you with my righteous right hand. (Isaiah 41:10)

Say to those with fearful hearts, "Be strong, and do not fear, for your God is coming to destroy your enemies. He is coming to save you." (Isaiah 35:4 NLT)

The LORD is my light and my salvation; whom shall I fear? The LORD is the stronghold of my life; of whom shall I be afraid? (Psalm 27:1)

In other words, the Bible teaches this: When your fears are big, turn your heart toward your even bigger God.

Of course, fearful thoughts may pop into your mind without your wanting them to be there. Everyone gets afraid. But when this happens, remember that the Lord is near. Ask him to help you, to remind you how much he loves you and how strong he is. When you are afraid, fear him.

MORE TO EXPLORE If you'd like to learn more about what God has promised his children, you may want to read *God's Promises (Making Him Known)* by Sally Michael.

22

HOW TO MEMORIZE ANYTHING

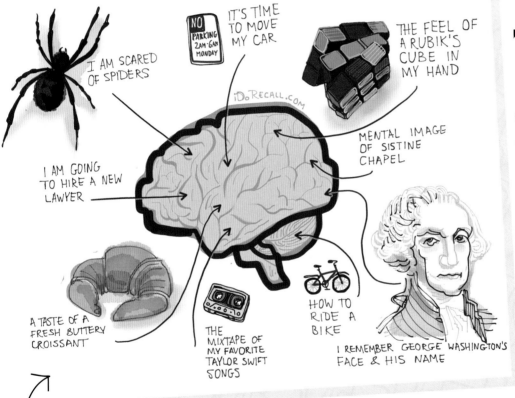

I AM SCARED OF SPIDERS

IT'S TIME TO MOVE MY CAR

NO PARKING 2AM-6AM MONDAY

THE FEEL OF A RUBIK'S CUBE IN MY HAND

iDoRecall.com

MENTAL IMAGE OF SISTINE CHAPEL

I AM GOING TO HIRE A NEW LAWYER

A TASTE OF A FRESH BUTTERY CROISSANT

THE MIXTAPE OF MY FAVORITE TAYLOR SWIFT SONGS

HOW TO RIDE A BIKE

I REMEMBER GEORGE WASHINGTON'S FACE & HIS NAME

"I can't remember the last time I forgot something."

Thinking time is not wasted time. God has always expected his people to use the minds he gave them. Over 100 times the Bible reminds you to think, to not forget, to remember. Some of these verses are on the next page.

So, what can you do to help things stick inside your brain? Some people (about 1 person out of 100) have a "photographic memory"—they basically remember everything they see. But most of us don't have such amazing minds; we have to find other ways to keep facts from draining out of our ears. Here are a few tips on how to remember things:

Combine unconnected facts. Think of your mind like a backpack. You wouldn't wear a backpack and then try to carry 30 other things in your arms. But if you put all those items into your backpack, you could carry everything at once.

It's easier to recall new facts when you connect them to things you already know. For example, do you remember the colors of the rainbow in the correct order? They are red, orange, yellow, green, blue, indigo, violet. But it's easier to remember if you combine the first letter of each color to form a name (Roy G. Biv) or a sentence: "Rabid oxen yanked grizzly bears into villages."

Imagine a picture. Here's another memory trick you can try. When trying to remember a person's name, connect that name with something you notice about the person. For example, a guy named Harry who had a bushy beard would be easy to remember. Or if you visualize a hat (or "lid") on someone named Lydia, then you'll be more likely to remember her name.

Hear, O Israel: The LORD our God, the LORD is one. You shall love the LORD your God with all your heart and with all your soul and with all your might. And these words that I command you today shall be on your heart. Deuteronomy 6:4–6

My son, do not forget my teaching, but let your heart keep my commandments. Proverbs 3:1

Remember Jesus Christ, risen from the dead. 2 Timothy 2:8

Do you not remember that . . . I told you these things? 2 Thessalonians 2:5

Remember the word that I said to you: "A servant is not greater than his master." John 15:20

And I will make every effort so . . . you may be able at any time to recall these things. 2 Peter 1:15

What is the shortest verse in the Bible?
"Jesus wept." (John 11:35)

Write it out. When it comes to memorizing Bible verses, for example, write out the verses on a card. Then write down just the first letter of each word on the back of the card. Don't try to memorize the list of letters. Instead, glance at the letters if you get stuck and can't remember what word comes next. The letters will automatically connect your mind to the words of the verse without giving you the complete verse.

Blessed is the man who walks not in the counsel of the wicked, nor stands in the way of sinners, nor sits in the seat of scoffers; but his delight is in the law of the LORD, and on his law he meditates day and night. He is like a tree planted by streams of water that yields its fruit in its season, and its leaf does not wither. In all that he does, he prospers. Psalm 1:1-3

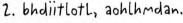

FRONT

BACK

Psalm 1:1-3

1. Bitmwwnitcotw, nsitwos, nsitsos;

2. bhdiitlotL, aohlhmdan.

3. Hilatpbsowtyifiis, aildnw. lathd, hp.

Don't forget to remember. After reading your Bible, you won't be able to recall everything that you read. But at least try to remember how God's Word answered the following questions:

• What is God like?
• What has God done for you?
• What has God promised you?

PSALM THINGS TO REMEMBER

If you're up to a challenge, try memorizing Psalm 1, Psalm 23, and Psalm 100. (See how long it takes you to memorize a psalm if you read it slowly, out loud, five times a day.)

What is the longest verse in the Bible?

Esther 8:9 has 80 words: "The king's scribes were summoned at that time, in the third month, which is the month of Sivan, on the twenty-third day. And an edict was written, according to all that Mordecai commanded concerning the Jews, to the satraps and the governors and the officials of the provinces from India to Ethiopia, 127 provinces, to each province in its own script and to each people in its own language, and also to the Jews in their script and their language."

23

GOD'S (NOT SO) SECRET MISSION

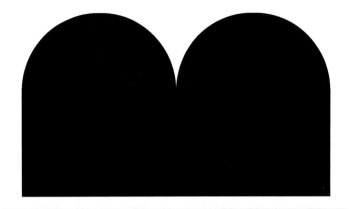

Did you know that today God is on an important mission? It's the same one he's had for a long time.

GOD'S TOP-PRIORITY MISSION: To spread his glory around the world so people from all nations can know and enjoy him.

At the beginning of history, God created Adam and Eve "in his image." That means that in some way they resembled God, the way people might say to you, "You look just like your mom (or dad)." God then commanded Adam and Eve to fill the earth with

people—children and grandchildren—who also resemble God (Genesis 1:27–28). They'd all join God on his mission to spread reflections of his glory around the world.

But Adam and Eve rejected God's mission. They decided not to follow or listen to God (the Bible calls this "sin") and ever since, things have been a mess. Every human since that time still reflects God's image, but we also display ourselves, going on our own little missions, not God's. And because of sin, other bad things have happened (and still happen!)—fights, lies, jealousy, wars, disease, death. Instead of the earth being filled with God's glory, it seemed to overflow with sin and suffering. But God had a surprising plan.

From everyone who lived on the earth, God picked one family to carry out his mission. Same mission, new start. God chose Abram (later known as Abraham) to become the head of a new people—God's own people. God would teach this new people what he was like and how to reflect that glory. God was going to use Abraham and his children to spread his glory and bring blessing to all nations of the world (Genesis 12:1–3).

Sadly, Abraham and his children (the Israelites) didn't display God clearly at all. Their reflection of God was covered with the grime and dirt of sin. Even though God told them how to live in a way that would reflect him, they disobeyed his law. Was God's mission doomed to fail?

No, it was all part of the plan. Many centuries passed

until one day an Israelite was born who always loved God and people completely. He always wanted to do things God's way. You could say he was a "new" Adam, because he was the perfect reflection of God. His name, of course, is Jesus.

Jesus is the One who accomplishes God's mission. He lived the life we could never live. He died the death we should have died. In dying he took away all the sin of God's people. When he rose from the dead he defeated death forever! And his resurrection is our guarantee that our sins are really forgiven. Because of Jesus's successful mission, all of his followers are now part of a new creation, reflecting his glory.

Even today Jesus commands his followers to take the blessing of God to every nation

WHAT IS GOD'S GLORY?

The "glory" of something is whatever sets it apart as special. The glory of Mount Everest is its height (no mountain is taller). The glory of a blue whale is its size (no animal is bigger).

Everest
Aconcagua
Denali

Then what is the glory of God? God's glory is the display of his "God-ness." No one else is God—he is in a class all by himself. And he is very, very good at being God. He is the most loving, most merciful, most gracious, most right.

Here is how God describes himself: "Yahweh! The Lord! The God of compassion and mercy! I am slow to anger and filled with unfailing love and faithfulness. I lavish unfailing love to a thousand generations. I forgive iniquity, rebellion, and sin. But I do not excuse the guilty" (Exodus 34:6–7 NLT).

So when God displays his glory, he is inviting you to see, admire, and enjoy what he is truly like: amazingly good, loving, gracious, and true.

Mount Everest

on earth (Matthew 28:18–20). And one day God will complete that mission. And "the dry land of earth will be filled with the knowledge of the glory of the Lord as the waters cover the sea" (Habakkuk 2:14 NLT).

When that happens, God's people will exclaim, "Mission accomplished!"

"Worthy are you to take the scroll and to open its seals, for you were slain, and by your blood you ransomed people for God from every tribe and language and people and nation, and you have made them a kingdom and priests to our God, and they shall reign on the earth." Revelation 5:9–10

❡   ❡   ❡

If you're one of God's children, he has a mission for *you*. It's his own mission—to reflect his glory and pass along the Good News about Jesus. Here are three simple suggestions of where you can start:

1. **Pray** (Ephesians 6:19; Colossians 4:3–4; Romans 10:1)

2. **Love people** (John 4:1–42; 13:34–35; Acts 16:13)

3. **Tell them about Jesus** (Matthew 28:19–20; Acts 8:4)

STARTING YOUR MISSION!

MORE TO EXPLORE ▶ Interested in reading more about people who joined God's secret mission? "Christian Heroes: Then and Now" is a series of biographies written by Janet and Geoff Benge. Here are a few good ones: *Samuel Zwemer: The Burden of Arabia; William Carey: Obliged to Go; Jim Elliot: One Great Purpose; Adoniram Judson: Bound for Burma.*

24

WOMEN WHO GAVE THEIR LIVES FOR CHRIST

AMY CARMICHAEL

Born in 1867, Amy Wilson Carmichael grew up in a Christian family in Ireland. She was the oldest child in a household with eight children. And although she was born with brown eyes, as a child Amy wished she had blue eyes.

Amy's eyes weren't her only problem. She suffered from neuralgia, a painful disease that affects the nerves of the body. Sometimes she couldn't leave the house for weeks. On top of this, when Amy was 18 years old her father died. Yet none of these things stopped Amy from helping the poor girls she saw going to work at the mills and factories of her city. They needed help, and they needed Jesus. So Amy started a Sunday morning class to teach the Good News to her girls. Over time her class grew until she was teaching over 500 people!

When she was 20 years old, Amy heard the preaching of
Hudson Taylor, the famous missionary to China. God used
his message to lead Amy to become a missionary. But she
didn't know *where* God would send her. At first she thought
God might be sending her to serve in China, but that didn't
work out. Then she traveled to Japan but became so sick that
she had to go back to Ireland. After that she even spent some
time as a missionary in Sri Lanka but became sick again. Yet
this time, she didn't go back home. Instead, she regained her
strength in the nearby country of India. And it was to this land
that God led her to spend the rest of her life as a missionary.

While in India, Amy once again saw young girls in need
of help and in need of Jesus. Often hurt and treated badly,
these girls were slaves in Hindu temples. One day a young
girl named Preena escaped from a temple and ran to Amy for

Amy helped young
slave girls in India

protection. Preena climbed onto Amy's lap and called her "Ammai," which means "Mother." Years later Preena talked about meeting Amy. She said:

"Our precious Ammai was having her morning meal. When she saw me, the first thing she did was to put me on her lap and kiss me. I thought, 'My mother used to put me on her lap and kiss me—who is this person who kisses me like my mother?' From that day she became my mother, body and soul."

Amy continued to help these slave girls, often putting her own life at risk to rescue them. Like a spy, Amy would disguise herself as a woman from India in order to sneak into the Hindu temples. She would dress in the traditional clothes of India and darken her skin with coffee in order to secretly rescue enslaved girls. And so it was that Amy came to realize that God had given her exactly the right colored eyes—the eye color most common to the Indian people—brown. Amy's brown eyes allowed her to blend in and go on her secret rescue missions. Blue eyes would have given away her true identity.

Soon Amy was caring for many young girls. And soon they too came to love Amy with all their heart. But life was not easy with so many mouths to feed and danger all around. Amy gave up her comfort, her friends, her plans, and her time. Once Amy received a letter from another woman who wanted to know what missionary life was like. Here is Amy's reply: "Missionary life is simply a chance to die." She was giving all of her life to follow Jesus, who said, "If anyone would come after me, let him deny himself and take up his cross and follow me" (Mark 8:34).

When Amy was about 65 years old, she fell, broke her leg, and hurt her back terribly. Her injuries meant she was to spend much of the last 19 years of her life in bed. Yet even these years of pain were spent ministering to other people. Amy wrote 16 books and rewrote ones she had written earlier. One of her most famous books has the simple title: *If*. It is a collection of devotional thoughts, each one ending with the same phrase: "then I know nothing of Calvary love." Here's a sampling.

If I ask to be delivered from trial rather than for deliverance out of it, to the praise of His glory; **if** I forget that the way of the Cross leads to the Cross and not to a bank of flowers; **if** I regulate my life on these lines, or even unconsciously my thinking, so that I am surprised when the way is rough and think it strange, though the word is, "Think it not strange, count it all joy," **then** I know nothing of Calvary love.

Amy died in India in 1951. She was 83 years old. Over her grave stands a birdbath. On it is written one word: "Ammai."

LOTTIE MOON

"I would I had a thousand lives that I might give them to . . . China!"
—*Lottie Moon*

These are the radical words of Charlotte ("Lottie") Moon, who was born in 1840 in Virginia. People remembered Lottie as a tiny girl, full of energy. She was also super-smart. She learned six foreign languages: Hebrew, Greek, Latin, Italian, French, and Spanish. She was raised in a Christian home, and turned to Jesus while she was in college. After that, every inch of her 4-foot, 3-inch frame was bent toward serving her Savior in missions.

So Lottie arrived on the coast of China hoping to share the gospel with Chinese women. Yet instead of traveling around China as an evangelist as she had hoped, Lottie found herself stuck inside a single classroom, teaching about forty unruly students.

But that didn't stop her. Even while serving as a teacher, Lottie longed to do *more* to spread the gospel. So she used her pen, writing dozens of letters and articles encouraging people to become missionaries. (The book of her compiled letters is over 400 pages!) And God used Lottie's strong words to shake many men and women into action for Christ. She wrote: "One cannot help asking sadly, why is the love of gold more potent than love of souls? The number of men mining and prospecting for gold in . . . [Shandong] is more than double the number of men representing [Christ]! What a lesson . . . to ponder."

Her writing helped start a yearly Christmas offering for missionaries, which in its first year collected $3,315, enough to send three missionaries to China. (Since then over $3 billion has been raised for missions.)

Eventually, Lottie was able to travel to the heartland of China where she was serving alone as a Christian witness. All day long she would work, speaking again and again about Jesus. Thousands came to hear her.

In 1889 she wrote, "I am trying honestly to do the work that could fill the hands of three or four women, and in addition must do much work that ought to be done by young men." With the exception of two trips home, Lottie would serve in China from the age of 33, in 1873, until she died in 1912 at the age of 72. She gave her life to serve Christ. In the century since her death, the energetic sacrifice of Lottie Moon has yielded much fruit for the Lord's cause.

Lottie was missionary in the heartland of China for over 39 years

MORE TO EXPLORE

To learn more about these women check out these biographies by Janet and Geoff Benge: *Amy Carmichael: Rescuer of Precious Gems* and *Lottie Moon: Giving Her All for China.*

LATIN WORDS YOU SHOULD KNOW

et cetera

About 60 percent of English words come from Latin, the 2,500-year-old language that the Caesars spoke in ancient Rome. Words such as *solar, lunar, mental,* and *regal* are based on Latin. Some Latin words and phrases never actually made it into English. Instead, we just say the word in the original Latin. You've probably heard someone use the word *et cetera,* which means "and so forth." They might say, "I bought lots of red-colored fruit at the grocery store today: apples, raspberries, cherries, strawberries, *et cetera.*"

Here are some common (and not so common) Latin words and phrases. Learn a few by heart. Then try them out in conversations with your friends, parents, and teachers.

Carpe diem

Bona fide: Genuine, sincere

My story is the *bona fide* truth.

Canis meus id comedit: My dog ate it

Carpe diem: Seize the day

Clamo, clamatis, omnes clamamus pro glace lactis: I scream; you scream; we all scream for ice cream

Credo: I believe

Deo volente: God willing

E pluribus unum: Out of many, one

The motto on the seal of the United States of America, the melting pot of many countries.

Et cetera (etc.): And so forth

Exempli gratia (e.g.): For example

People arrived in lots of different vehicles (*e.g.,* sports cars, trucks, motorcycles, and minivans).

Fac ut gaudeam: Make my day!

Gloria in excelsis deo: Glory to God in the highest

Id est (i.e.): That is

The child showed his displeasure (*i.e.,* he screamed for 20 minutes).

Labra lege: Read my lips

Noli habere bovis, vir: Don't have a cow, man!

Per se: Taken alone

He reads books, but he's not an expert in literature *per se*.

Postatem obscuri lateris nescitis: You do not know the power of the dark side

Semper fidelis: Always faithful

The United States Marine Corps motto.

Sic: Thus; used in books to show a mistake

This sentence has a mistake in it but its *[sic]* on purpose.

Sine qua non: An essential thing; without which not

The quarterback was the *sine qua non* of the team's offense.

Sit vis nobiscum: May the force be with you

Sola deo Gloria: Glory to God alone

Sola gratia: By grace alone

Solo Christo: By Christ alone

Status quo: The existing condition

Verbatim: Exactly as said

Vice versa: The order being reversed

26

ROCK ON!
(JEWELS IN THE BIBLE)

ON THAT DAY THE LORD
THEIR GOD WILL RESCUE
HIS PEOPLE, JUST AS
A SHEPHERD RESCUES
HIS SHEEP. THEY WILL
SPARKLE IN HIS LAND
LIKE JEWELS IN A
CROWN.
ZECHARIAH 9:16 NLT

Scientists have identified 48 different kinds of precious stones or gems. Some of the most famous and valuable are diamonds, rubies, and emeralds. Recently, a very wealthy father bought his little daughter the Blue Moon diamond—for $48.5 million. That was some birthday present!

If you had been a king or queen in Bible times, you would probably have been super rich! You would have owned the "crown jewels," which were passed down from one king or queen to the next. This was called the treasure of the kingdom.

But in addition to this royal treasure, you would also have had your own personal treasure—bags of money, works of art, mansions, and jewelry. Your personal treasure would mean more to you than the treasure of the kingdom because it belonged only to

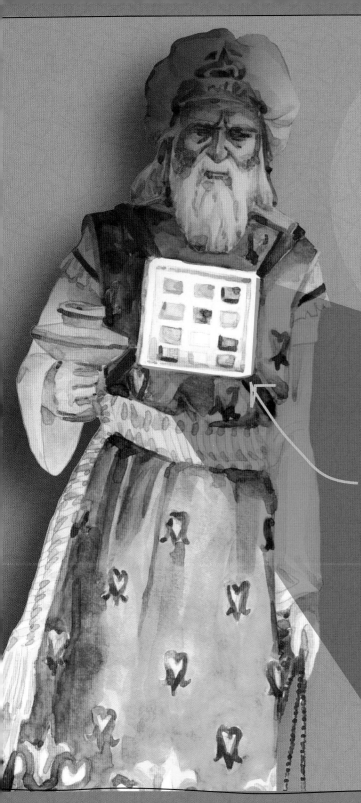

The Bible mentions many kinds of jewels. In fact, in the Old Testament, the high priest's breastplate had twelve gemstones, arranged in four rows of three. On each stone was written the name of one of the twelve tribes of Israel. As the high priest served in the Lord's presence in the Temple, he came representing all of God's people—those loved and valued by God as his precious treasure.

The book of Exodus identifies each gemstone on the high priest's breastplate.

"A row of sardius, topaz, and carbuncle shall be the first row; and the second row an emerald, a sapphire, and a diamond; and the third row a jacinth, an agate, and an amethyst; and the fourth row a beryl, an onyx, and a jasper. They shall be set in gold filigree. There shall be twelve stones with their names according to the names of the sons of Israel. They shall be like signets, each engraved with its name, for the twelve tribes."

Exodus 28:17—21

> BUT YOU ARE A CHOSEN RACE, A ROYAL PRIESTHOOD, A HOLY NATION, A PEOPLE FOR HIS OWN POSSESSION, THAT YOU MAY PROCLAIM THE EXCELLENCIES OF HIM WHO CALLED YOU OUT OF DARKNESS INTO HIS MARVELOUS LIGHT.
>
> 1 PETER 2:9

you—it was your *special* treasure.

The Bible says that it's the same way with God. He is the King of the universe. He owns it all: every planet, every nation, every gold mine, every jewel, every animal, every person. Yet did you know that God also has a "special treasure"? It's what he protects and values more than anything else he created. God's people are his special treasure—the jewels he loves most. If you belong to God, *you* are his special treasure. More than all else, he treasures his people (Deuteronomy 7:6; Titus 2:14).

That means that as a Christian you don't have to work to make God like you more. And so, you don't have to do stuff to make other people like you more. You don't have to look and act perfect. Because to God, you are a jewel that he already treasures. If you belong to Jesus, you are God's prized possession, his special treasure. Even more than diamonds and rubies and emeralds, *Christians* are the jewels of the Bible.

WHY CAN'T I?!

"Why can't I watch that TV show?"

"Why can't I listen to that music?"

"Why can't I download this app?"

"Why can't I wear these clothes?"

"Why can't I go to my friend's house?"

"Why can't I play this video game?"

Do your parents hear any of these complaints around your house? You probably already know that God wants you to obey your parents' rules (Ephesians 6:1–3). But have you ever tried to understand *why* your parents give permission for some things and not others? Here are some questions they may think about before they tell you yes or no:

1. Does the Bible talk about this? If yes, then we need to obey the Bible. **For example:** Is it OK to use bad words? (See Ephesians 5:4.)

2. What is good about this? Remember, God made the world "very good." Even though Adam and Eve's sin brought evil into God's world, the creation is still full of goodness. For example, some kinds of dancing are sinful, yet dancing itself still reflects some of God's original goodness. God gave dancing as a good way to express joy with our whole body. (Verses to read: Psalm 30:11; 149:3)

3. **Can we thank God for this?** God wants us to be able to give him thanks for everything he made for us to enjoy. (This is why we pray and offer thanks before meals.) If we cannot thank God from our hearts for something, then we shouldn't do it. **For example:** if you cannot bow your head and thank God for allowing you to enjoy a certain TV show, then you shouldn't watch it. (Verses to read: Romans 14:6; 1 Corinthians 10:30–31; 1 Timothy 4:3–5)

4. **Is this wise to do?** Some things may be just fine, but they may not be appropriate for a specific time or place. For example, there's nothing wrong with eating candy, but can you think of situations where it wouldn't be wise? (**For example:** eating *too much* candy or eating candy if you have health problems or eating sugar right before bedtime.) Parents may not allow you to read some book, watch certain movies, buy an expensive app, or wear a kind of outfit—not because all these things are wicked, but because they're not wise. Some choices just aren't appropriate for some ages or situations. (Verses to read: Proverbs 26:4 & 5; 1 Corinthians 10:23–24; Colossians 4:5)

5. Has this become too important? At its heart, sin is loving something that God made more than God who made it. Of course, God wants us to enjoy what he's made, but he wants us to enjoy him most of all. If we love even a good thing too much, it becomes for us a bad thing. **For example:** when you want to play a video game for hours and hours (and are rude to your family and neglect your chores around the house), then the game has become *too important* to you. It might not be a bad game, but it's become wrong for you because you love it too much. (Verses to read: 1 John 2:16; Colossians 3:5)

6. Does this make sin look normal? Certain things are evil because they make sin seem *innocent*. **For example:** characters in movies or books almost always show some sinful behavior or attitudes. Yet some movies or books make those wicked things seem perfectly fine or even funny. Everyone laughs or maybe no one even notices, and sin has now become common and comfortable. But in reality God hates sin. It brings destruction into people's lives, rips their relationships, and leads to death. Sin is *not* normal; it is not part of God's good plan for this world. (Verse to read: Romans 6:6)

THINK ABOUT IT

We have somehow got hold of the idea that error is only that which is outrageously wrong; and we do not seem to understand that the most dangerous person of all is the one who does not emphasize the right things.

—Martyn Lloyd-Jones

28

THE SECRET TO GROWING UP

Grown-ups get to do cool stuff: stay up late, drive cars, drink coffee, finish school, and go on adventures. But to be a grown-up, there's more you need to know. The secret to growing up is *knowing how to properly relate to God, other people, the created world, and yourself*. The Bible calls all this proper relating, "wisdom."

This sounds easy enough, but there's a problem. Ever since Adam and Eve rebelled against God (Genesis 3), no one has ever fully and rightly related to God, others, this world, and his or her own person.

No one, except one Man: Jesus Christ personally embodied the fullest expression of wise living (Luke 2:40–52; 11:29–32). Jesus is the most grown-up human ever (Ephesians 4:13). And if you are a Christian, if you are *in him*, "Jesus Christ has become to us wisdom from God" (1 Corinthians

THE ROAD

1:30; also see chapter 57, "Knots You Can't Untie"). Because Jesus is our wisdom, all Christians have now been restored to a right relationship with God forever.

So for the Christian, growing up means first learning to rely on Jesus as your wisdom and then understanding how to relate to people, situations, and yourself in wise ways. But you don't gain this kind of wisdom overnight. The pathway of wisdom is walked, not sprinted. Thankfully, God has described the pathway of wisdom for us. Proverbs 2 provides a map, telling young Christians where to start their journey down this road of wisdom.

*   *   *

1. Accept the Wisdom You Have
(Proverbs 2:1–2)

Starting when you're very young, you should listen to the teaching of your parents— welcome their wisdom. Parents, especially Christian parents, will help you learn about God's Word and about the world around you. Open your ears and fill your heart with their wise words. (Other verses to read: Proverbs 9:6; 23:19)

F WISDOM

2. Seek the Wisdom You Lack (Proverbs 2:3–4)

As you grow up, start seeking wisdom yourself. Pray for wisdom. Praying like this is a vital part of your treasure hunt for wisdom, whose value exceeds gold or silver. If you need wisdom, then seek wisdom. Ask God for it. He is the Source of true wisdom. (Other verses to read: Proverbs 3:14; James 1:5)

3. Gain the Wisdom You Need (Proverbs 2:5–8)

When you pray for wisdom, the Lord gives you what you need to become wise. He will give you the fear of the LORD, which is the first and key ingredient to gaining a wise perspective for yourself. This means he will help you to know that he is the Boss of your life and you are not. Without the fear of the LORD, wise living is impossible.

4. Own the Wisdom You Know (Proverbs 2:9–10)

When you've received these ingredients of wisdom, then you will begin to understand every good path. This means that wisdom will live in your own heart. And this kind of wisdom will change you—so that you actually enjoy God's wise ways. Then the wisdom you've heard from others will become your own.

All this is the pathway of wisdom, the secret to growing up in God's good yet sin-twisted world.

🦶 🦶 🦶

How many proverbs (wise sayings) and songs did Solomon write?

3,000 proverbs and 1,005 songs (1 Kings 4:32)

How many horses did Solomon have?

12,000 horses (1 Kings 10:26)

If you're a Christian, Proverbs will teach you how to grow up, how to relate wisely. Here's a simple way to begin learning wisdom from this great book of the Bible. Since there are 31 chapters in Proverbs, you might want to read whichever chapter in Proverbs matches the day of the month.

But don't be discouraged or surprised when you stumble on the path of wisdom. Everyone does. Yet even when you fail and make foolish choices, God has provided the wisdom you need. Remember, Jesus Christ has become our true wisdom from God (1 Corinthians 1:30). He has already put you in right relationship to God, and when you ask him, he will also teach you how to live wisely (James 1:5).

Want to be treated like a grown-up? Ask the Lord to help you learn and live in wisdom—and dive into the book of Proverbs.

HAPPY IS THE PERSON WHO FINDS WISDOM AND GAINS UNDERSTANDING. FOR THE PROFIT OF WISDOM IS BETTER THAN SILVER, AND HER WAGES ARE BETTER THAN GOLD.

PROVERBS 3:13–14 NLT

29

WILD, WILDER, WILDEST

The wild ox (or aurochs) became extinct in the early 1600s. These powerful oxen sometimes reached 6-feet tall!

Tales of monsters and other wild creatures fill mythology. Ancient Greek myths speak of many fierce creatures. The Minotaur (a monster with the body of a man and the head of a bull) and Hydra (a many-headed serpent) are only two in a long list. The savage giant, Grendel, terrorizes the land in the Old English epic poem *Beowulf*. The modern English mythology of J. R. R. Tolkien's *The Hobbit* and *The Lord of the Rings* includes Smaug the dragon, Azog the orc, a Balrog, and the Nazgul.

The Bible too has its share of wild things. The end of the book

 How many times are dogs mentioned in the Bible?

Answer: 41 times

of Job presents a virtual zoo (38:39—41:34). The list starts off small. The first creatures are simply untamed animals, like the lion, hawk, and wild ox. The Bible makes the point that even wild creatures are part of God's animal kingdom. And he cares for them just like all the other animals. God feeds them; gives them offspring; and meets their needs—just like he does for a cute puppy or gentle panda.

Then Job goes on to mentions monster-like creatures. You can read about two monsters in Job 40:15—41:34. One of the creatures has a name that means super-beast—"Behemoth." The other monster is named Leviathan, which means something like "wraith." You wouldn't want to have to defend yourself against either of these!

But why do these monsters show up in the book of Job? God's point is that while we can't control many wild creatures, God can; he always has them on his leash. Because this is true, we can also depend on something else: God is always in control. He has control of even the wildest *situation*. As King of the universe, God controls everything: beasts, tornadoes, sickness, demons, accidents, etc. He's always making all things work together for his good—and his good is our good, too (Romans 8:28).

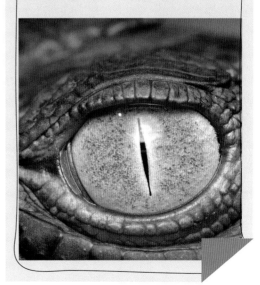

Did You KNOW?

Some think the behemoth may have been a hippopotamus—one of the most dangerous animals in modern-day Africa. The leviathan may have been a massive crocodile or wild sea creature. Others think these two "monsters" may have been dinosaurs.

How many times are cats mentioned in the Bible?

Answer: Lions and leopards are mentioned, but cats, never.

Here are some other wild creatures mentioned in the Bible:

Bats (Leviticus 11:19)

Bears (Isaiah 11:7)

Cobras (Isaiah 11:8)

Foxes (Nehemiah 4:3)

Hornets (Joshua 24:12)

Leopards (Jeremiah 5:6)

Lions (Psalm 10:9)

Lizards (Leviticus 11:30)

Nighthawks (Deuteronomy 14:15)

Oxen (Deuteronomy 33:17)

Porcupines (Isaiah 34:11)

Rats (Leviticus 11:29)

Scorpions (Luke 11:12)

Sea monsters (Job 7:12)

Snakes (Ecclesiastes 10:8)

Vultures (Leviticus 11:13)

Wild boars (Psalm 80:13)

Wild goats (Deuteronomy 14:5)

Wolves (Ezekiel 22:27)

MORE TO EXPLORE A couple of great stories that include some monsters are *100 Cupboards* (Book 1 of the 100 Cupboards Series) by N. D. Wilson; and *On the Edge of the Dark Sea of Darkness* (Book 1 of The Wingfeather Saga) by Andrew Peterson.

Completely Irrelephant

Elephants are not in the Bible, but they make for excellent jokes. Try these out on your friends and family, but be sure to tell them in this order.

Q: **What do you shoot a blue elephant with?**

A: A blue elephant gun

Q: **What do you shoot a white elephant with?**

A: ("A white elephant gun?") No, you hold its nose until it turns blue, and shoot it with a blue elephant gun.

Q: **How can you tell if there's been an elephant in the kitchen?**

A: There's a set of footprints in the peanut butter.

Q: **How many elephants can fit into a sports car?**

A: Four—two in the front, two in the back

Q: **How can you tell if there have been two elephants in the kitchen?**

A: There are two sets of footprints in the peanut butter.

Q: **Why did the elephant paint his toenails red?**

A: So he could hide in the cherry tree.

Q: **How can you tell if there have been three elephants in the kitchen?**

A: There are three sets of footprints in the peanut butter.

Q: **Do you know how Tarzan died?**

A: Picking cherries

Q: **How can you tell if there have been four elephants in the kitchen?**

A: There's a sports car parked out back.

MIND YOUR MANNERS

Madison (age 9): "Who cares about good manners, anyway?!"

Josh (age 11): "Manners are dumb—they're just some silly rules that somebody made up!"

It's true; manners do look like rules that don't mean anything. After all, kids in other countries don't have the same rules as you do, right? Does it *really* matter if you put your elbows on the table? Or that you spread your napkin on your lap during meals? Or that you write thank-you notes? Yes and no. Manners matter because people matter.

For example, it's true that God never commands you to not interrupt when your friends are talking. You could be a perfectly good Christian and just jump into a conversation whenever you want. No Bible rule against that. But if you keep interrupting, you won't have as much fun with your friends (and they may avoid you in the future). However, if you listen to your friends before starting to talk, then you and your friends can have a good time together. This is the way manners work.

Manners may not be listed in the Bible—and they're certainly not the most important things in life—but they do allow people to enjoy and help each other. Imagine what would happen if people only focused on their phones and completely ignored everyone around them? If every person at dinner always reached across the table to grab some food? If someone was super noisy in the next room when you were trying to sleep?

The rules that guide this kind of behavior aren't important in themselves, and they don't even have to make sense. But Jesus taught that people are important (Matthew 22:34–40), and that's why we use good manners.

🍪　🍪　🍪

As a Christian, having good manners won't make God love you any more than he already does. But it is a way to show his love to others. **Here are some manners you can use to serve and enjoy people you know:**

* Enter a room listening, not talking.

* If something doesn't belong to you, don't touch it.

* Look for opportunities to be helpful; move toward (not away from) whoever needs help.

* When you talk to others, look them in the eye and take interest in them.

* Don't call attention to yourself by showing off.

* If you don't know what to do, ask.

* If you are calling out for someone and they don't answer you, wait or go find them. Don't just yell.

* Don't just sit there while people around you are standing or working. Join them.

* Always leave a place in better condition than when you entered. Clean as you go.

* Think ahead. Try to see the results of your actions before you do them.

* Guests and friends always have the first choice of toys and games.

* Do what you *should* first, before doing what you *want*.

* Take humble responsibility for your behavior; you cannot make excuses and progress at the same time.

* Fun is only fun when everyone is having fun.

* When you are bored, there's a good chance you are being self-centered.

* If you have to push to get somewhere, wait or go around.

* Say please and thank you and excuse me, whenever appropriate.

Did You KNOW?

Good manners change over time.

In America in the 1950s, it was common for men, who often wore hats then, to take them off when they entered a building or started talking to a woman. In that same time period, parents often told their children that they should only "speak when you're spoken to." That meant, don't start a conversation with a grown-up; wait for them to talk to you first. Different time period, different manners.

Manners also change depending on where you live. In parts of Europe chewing gum in public is considered bad manners. (In fact, in Singapore it's illegal!) And in much of the Far East, sitting with your feet pointed toward someone else is offensive, while belching after a meal is a way to compliment the chef.

31

EXPLORE NEW WORLDS

Come exploring with two British authors who, over the years, have captivated and delighted readers. They are John Bunyan and C. S. Lewis. For millions of children and grown-ups, the tales of Bunyan and Lewis have opened a doorway to new worlds and new adventures.

THE DANGEROUS JOURNEY

John Bunyan, born in Britain in 1628, is best known for his allegory *The Pilgrim's Progress*. An allegory is a story in which the people and plot stand for ideas about life. For example, in *Pilgrim's Progress*, a character named "Mr. Talkative," represents someone who talks a lot, but does very little.

In *Pilgrim's Progress* the author narrates a dream about a man named Christian, who flees his hometown, the City of Destruction, and goes in search of the Celestial City. Along the way Christian encounters many people—some good, some bad—in addition to battles, giants, dragons, and danger at every turn. It's a story about Christian, but it also represents the story of every Christian. This is how Bunyan starts the story:

> As I walked through the wilderness of this world, I lighted on a certain place where was a Den, and I laid me down in that place to sleep: and, as I slept, I dreamed a dream. I dreamed, and behold, I saw a man clothed with rags, standing in a certain place, with his face from his own house, a book in his hand, and a great burden upon his back. I looked, and saw him open the book, and read therein; and, as he read, he wept, and trembled; and, not being able longer to contain, he brake out with a lamentable cry, saying, "What shall I do?"

Bunyan wrote this book over 300 years ago, so the wording can be a little hard to understand. But you can read versions of the book written in modern English. Here are some good ones:

- *Dangerous Journey* (a shorter version with illustrations, edited by Oliver Hunkin)

- *Little Pilgrim's Progress* (a simplified version, edited by Helen Taylor)

- *Pilgrim's Progress* (a brilliant modern retelling, with illustrations, by Gary Schmidt)

Less well known is Bunyan's allegory *Holy War*. In this story, the city of Mansoul is under attack by a terrible enemy, Diabolus. The citizens must uncover the enemy's plans and defeat him. (In other words, this story tells how Satan tempts Christians to sin and how we can resist those temptations.) *The War for Mansoul* is a good modern version of Bunyan's book, adapted by Ethel Barrett. (If you'd like to learn more about John Bunyan, check out "More Men Who Gave Their Lives for Christ," page 147.)

THE LAND OF NARNIA

Clive Staples (C. S.) Lewis, known to his friends as "Jack," was born in 1898 and died in 1963, on the same day that another famous "Jack" died: US President John F. Kennedy. As a boy, Lewis disliked being called Clive, preferring instead to be called "Jack" (perhaps after a family dog named Jacksie).

For most of his life, Lewis was an author and a professor of literature at both Cambridge University and Oxford University in England. Like Bunyan, Lewis didn't believe in God as a young man. Then one day God opened Jack's heart—first to know that God really existed and then to trust God's Son as his Savior. You can read more about how Jack grew up and came to believe in Christ in his autobiography, *Surprised by Joy.*

After becoming a Christian, Jack and some others

formed a club for writers they called "The Inklings." (One of these friends was J. R. R. Tolkien, author of *The Hobbit* and *The Lord of the Rings*.) And for many years, Jack thought and spoke about how Jesus was real and how Christianity was true. He wrote about this in a great book: *Mere Christianity*.

Jack is best remembered for writing the seven books in *The Chronicles of Narnia*. In these magical tales, you'll meet four children (Peter, Susan, Edmund, and Lucy who are brothers and sisters) along with others, who all enjoy exciting adventures throughout the land of Narnia. In these books, Lewis made the biblical stories of the creation of the universe, the sin of Adam and Eve, the crucifixion and resurrection of Jesus, and more, come alive to the imagination.

Every reader of the *Narnia* series has some favorite characters (my son's are Prince Caspian from Book 4

Did You KNOW?

OUT OF THIS WORLD DISCOVERY

In 2003, a British scholar named Michael Ward uncovered a mystery about *The Chronicles of Narnia* that had been hidden for over fifty years. One night he was reading a poem that C. S. Lewis had written about the seven planets known to the ancient world, entitled "The Heavens." In the middle of the poem, one phrase, about the planet Jupiter, leapt off the page: "Winter past and guilt forgiven." Here, Ward realized, was a perfect summary of *The Lion, the Witch, and the Wardrobe*.

Michael Ward's mind began whirling: there are seven planets known in the ancient world (which included the sun and moon), and there are seven books in the Narnia series. These thoughts started an avalanche of study and discovery. It seems that Lewis had hidden clues all throughout the series that connect each of the seven Narnia books with a "planet." (Read the upside down text after each title below to see which one fits which planet.)

Here's a list of the seven books of *The Chronicles*, in the order in which the events in the stories occur. However, it's best to read the books in the order in which they were published (see the dates following the titles).

The Magician's Nephew (1955) (Venus)

The Lion, the Witch and the Wardrobe (1950) (Jupiter)

The Horse and His Boy (1954) (Mercury)

Prince Caspian (1951) (Mars)

The Voyage of the Dawn Treader (1952) (the Sun)

The Silver Chair (1953) (the Moon)

The Last Battle (1956) (Saturn)

MORE TO EXPLORE If you'd like to know more about Narnia and the planets, you can read *The Narnia Code: C. S. Lewis and the Secret of the Seven Heavens* by Michael Ward.

C. S. Lewis wrote:

"The Christian does not think God will love us because we are good, but that God will make us good because He loves us."
(Mere Christianity)

"Eating and reading are two pleasures that combine admirably." (Surprised by Joy)

"Humility is not thinking less of yourself, it's thinking of yourself less."
(Mere Christianity)

"If we find ourselves with a desire that nothing in this world can satisfy, the most probable explanation is that we were made for another world."
(The Weight of Glory)

and Jewel, the faithful, fierce, and magnificent unicorn, in Book 7). But in every book, Lewis focuses our attention on one primary character—the one who represents Jesus Christ—a good, but not tame lion named Aslan.

If you've already read The Chronicles of Narnia and want to enjoy more adventures with "Jack," then you may want to read his Space Trilogy. Written for older ages, these science fiction books carry you all over the galaxy with the books' hero, Elwin Ransom. Like The Chronicles of Narnia, these space adventures also retell stories and truths from the Bible. And some people think these three books (Out of the Silent Planet, Perelandra, and That Hideous Strength) are even better than The Chronicles of Narnia.

MORE TO EXPLORE If you'd like to learn more about how God has changed the lives of other people, you may want to read Case for Grace for Kids by Lee Strobel with Robert Suggs and Robert Elmer.

32

WHAT IS GOD LIKE ?

A s you grow up, there are thousands of things you have to learn. You have to learn how to brush your teeth (*up and down, not side to side*). How to make your bed. How to ride a bike. How to read a book (*important*). How to put a rubber band around the spray nozzle at the kitchen sink (*not really important, but fun . . . at least once*).

It's good to know most of these things. **But there is only one thing you must know: you must know God. He's not just an important part of your life; he *is* your life.**

But what is God like? No living human being has ever seen the Father face to face. And no one is still alive who saw and heard Jesus during his earthly lifetime 2,000 years ago.

So, if you've never seen God, how can you possibly know what he's like? And how could you ever get to know him personally? The short answer is that you can ask him to show himself to you. The Bible teaches that every person who asks, seeks, and knocks because they want to know God, will be answered. (Here's the longer answer: When Jesus left earth and returned to the Father, he gave his people the best gift of all—his Spirit. His Spirit shows us how much we need God, reminds us of God's love for us, and shows us what God is really like. Jesus told his disciples and us all about his Spirit in the book of John, especially the section from chapters 14–16. Still today, when you turn to Jesus in faith and ask for forgiveness for your sins, he gives you himself—his own Spirit to live inside of you. And the Spirit of Jesus will teach you all about God.)

The main way the Spirit teaches us what God is like is through the Bible. The Bible is God's Word to his people, and in the Bible are vivid word pictures showing us exactly what God is like.

Here are some of the self-portraits God has used to tell us about himself.

 ## GOD IS OUR FATHER

The Lord is like a father to his children, tender and compassionate to those who fear him. (Psalm 103:13 NLT)

God protects and provides for his children. In fact, it's not just something he does—it is who he is. He has always been a Father. And his fatherhood is not merely part of him: he's Father through all his person, in all he does, and through all time. Before the world was made, he was Father to the Son (Jesus Christ). God *is* Father; the perfect Father.

 GOD IS OUR JUDGE

"Should not the Judge of all the earth do what is right?" (Genesis 18:25b NLT)

God, the Judge, hates sin. He hates anything that harms his children. He always does the right thing. Not because he's trying to obey some rules. But because that's what he's like: always totally right and just and fair.

 GOD IS OUR SUN

For the LORD God is our sun and our shield. He gives us grace and glory. (Psalm 84:11a NLT)

The earth's natural life is fueled by the sun's energy, the star at the center of our solar system. Its light and heat nourish life on earth. Similarly, God is the ultimate source of our life, the center of our lives. And he supplies all we need: love, forgiveness, food, clothing, etc.

 GOD IS OUR SHELTER

But you are a tower of refuge to the poor, O LORD, a tower of refuge to the needy in distress. You are

 THINK ABOUT IT

"A little knowledge of God is worth more than a great deal of knowledge about him." J. I. Packer

It's easy to get so busy knowing facts about God, that you forget about knowing God himself. In his most famous book, *Knowing God*, J. I. (James Innell) Packer (born in 1926) has helped millions of believers focus on God—hearing him, trusting him, following him, worshiping him.

Packer teaches that knowing God (and being known by him), like you would know one of your friends, is much more valuable than knowing lots of facts about him.

a refuge from the storm and a shelter from the heat. (Isaiah 25:4a NLT)

Ever since Adam and Eve sinned and had to leave the Garden of Eden, life has been difficult. Doing homework is hard; making and keeping friends is hard; saying "I was wrong" is hard; obeying your mom or dad is hard. And, like working out in the scorching sun, at times we need a break in the shade. God says, "When life is hard, turn to me. Let me be your relief: I am your shelter from the heat."

 ## JESUS IS THE LAMB

"Behold, the Lamb of God, who takes away the sin of the world!" (John 1:29b)

In the Old Testament, sinners sacrificed lambs as a picture of God punishing and forgiving their sin. These lambs were just animals; they couldn't really take someone's punishment. But Jesus is *the* Lamb sent from God. And his death really, truly removes the sin of all who trust him.

 ## JESUS IS THE LION

"Stop weeping! Look, the Lion of the tribe of Judah, the heir to David's throne, has won the victory." (Revelation 5:5b NLT)

Jesus is the Lamb, who was sacrificed, and he's the conquering Lion. The king of beasts represents the raw and majestic strength of the King of kings. He, and only he, is mighty and able to accomplish all of God's good plans for this world. Nothing can stop this lion, for as C. S. Lewis wrote, "He is not a tame lion."

 # JESUS IS THE VINE

"I am the true grapevine, and my Father is the gardener. He cuts off every branch of mine that doesn't produce fruit, and he prunes the branches that do bear fruit so they will produce even more." (John 15:1–2 NLT)

Jesus is the source of life for every Christian. He is the vine, and we're the branches that sprout off this vine. Being connected to him is how we live and grow. We cannot please God apart from Jesus. We need Jesus for everything we do as Christians.

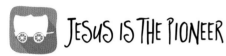 # JESUS IS THE PIONEER

This hope is a strong and trustworthy anchor for our souls. It leads us through the curtain into God's inner sanctuary. Jesus has already gone in there for us. (Hebrews 6:19–20a NLT)

Jesus has already left this fallen earth and gone to the Father. But he didn't shut the door behind himself. Instead, he's propped open the door for his people. Like a pioneer, he has blazed a trail for us to follow. And if we are connected to Jesus, we know that since he made it safely to the Father, we will too.

 # THE HOLY SPIRIT IS LIKE THE WIND

"The wind blows wherever it wants. Just as you can hear the wind but can't tell where it comes from or where it is going, so you can't explain how people are born of the Spirit." (John 3:8 NLT)

The Bible word, "spirit" is the same word as "breath" or "wind." In a storm you might see a tree bending and say, "Look at the wind!" But you're not really seeing the wind; you're seeing what the wind is doing. So it is with the Spirit of God. The Holy Spirit secretly accomplishes God's work on earth. He moves and you can't see how he is working. But quietly, invisibly, God is bending people to his good will.

 ## THE HOLY SPIRIT IS LIKE A BIRD

In the beginning God created the heavens and the earth. The earth was formless and empty, and darkness covered the deep waters. And the Spirit of God was hovering over the surface of the waters. (Genesis 1:1–2 NLT)

Have you ever seen a picture of a mother bird, spreading her wings over her nest of eggs? She's brooding or hovering over her unhatched chicks. She's bringing warmth and protection. She's nurturing them into a new life. In a similar way, the Holy Spirit brooded over this planet in the beginning, bringing creation to life. And he continues to bring spiritual life to humans who are dead in sin.

 ## THE HOLY SPIRIT IS LIKE A HELPER

"And I will ask the Father, and he will give you another Helper, to be with you forever, even the Spirit of truth, whom the world cannot receive, because it neither sees him nor knows him. You know him, for he dwells with you and will be in you." (John 14:16–17)

During the few years Jesus lived on earth, he taught and encouraged his friends. He was their helper. But what would they do when Jesus went back to the Father? Who would help them then? Jesus promised that he would send the Holy Spirit to take his place, to be their new helper. And to this day, the Spirit still helps, teaches, encourages, and strengthens God's people.

 ## THE HOLY SPIRIT IS LIKE OIL

So as David stood there among his brothers, Samuel took the flask of olive oil he had brought and anointed David with the oil. And the Spirit of the Lord came powerfully upon David from that day on. (1 Samuel 16:13 NLT)

The prophet Samuel took some oil and poured it on young David, anointing him to be king one day. This showed that he was chosen by God to do a special job. The Spirit came on David, giving him the power to do what God asked of him. And even today, the Spirit is like this anointing oil, giving all Christians the power to do what God asks of them.

33

CAN YOU PROVE THAT GOD EXISTS?

It depends what you mean by "prove." You can't take a picture of God and show it to your friends, but his "fingerprints" are everywhere. The existence of God, whom we can't see, is the best explanation for the world that we can see. Of course you see the Lord most clearly by reading his Word, but if you look carefully at the world around you, you can't miss him.

BOOKS, PLAYS, AND MOVIES

Have you ever noticed how often books, plays, and movies tell stories that remind you of Jesus's life? It's as if the human heart were created with the need and the desire for a rescuer, a king, a friend. The following characters all resemble the kind of person we long for, the kind only truly found in Jesus:

the Lone ranger, who fights for what's right although often mistaken for a criminal

superman, who comes into the world as a baby and fights to rid the world of evil

hiccup, from *How to Train Your Dragon,* who overcomes evil through humility and gentleness

the iron giant, who saves others by sacrificing himself

balto, who was despised and rejected but still gives everything to rescue those in need

sydney carton, from *Tale of Two Cities*, who gives his life in the place of another

jean valjean, from *Les Misérables*, who spends his life showing mercy to the undeserving

aslan, from *The Chronicles of Narnia*, who sacrifices his life for the sin of someone else

frodo, from *The Lord of the Rings*, who in weakness bears the burden of evil to save the world

mufasa, from *The Lion King*, who gives his life to rescue his child

anna, from *Frozen*, who, in an act of true love, sacrifices herself for the undeserving, bringing life to the world

optimus prime, from *Transformers*, who fights and dies to save the world and is resurrected

NOW SHOWING

GOD IN THE ARTS
NARNIA   LORD OF THE RINGS
FROZEN   THE LION KING   TRANSFORM

131

ANCIENT HISTORY AND SOCIAL STUDIES

We know the creation and flood accounts in Genesis, but other ancient cultures also had creation and flood stories with features similar to the ones in Genesis. The real story, which the Bible records, had once been known throughout the ancient world.

In 1849, archaeologist Austen Henry Layard discovered clay tablets from ancient Babylon that contained a creation story known as the *Enuma Elish*. This pagan account of creation shares the following elements with the true story recorded in Genesis 1 and 2:

- Darkness exists before creation
- Light shines before the sun, moon, and stars are created
- Water is divided into two parts: waters above and waters below
- After creating waters, land, planets, and people—there is rest.

Other ancient documents tell of a flood that destroyed much of the world. The most famous account is the *Epic of Gilgamesh*. But there seem to be ancient flood stories within cultures all around the world, including: Arcadian, Assyrian, Celtic, Chaldean, Egyptian, German, Greek, Inuit, Lithuanian, Maori, Persian, Roman, Russian, Samoan, Scandinavian, Sumerian, Transylvanian, Turkish, and Welsh—and the list could go on.

❧ ❧ ❧

In his book, *Eternity in Their Hearts*, missionary Don Richardson tells how people in different places and times have given common evidence of one, true God.

• Many people groups believe in one divine being, the Creator of everything. Here's a sampling: the **Incas** of South America, the **Santal** of India, the **Gedeo** of Ethiopia, and the **Mbaka** of central Africa.

For example, in the 1920s, one member of the Mbaka tribe spoke of this one true Creator, called "Koro." He said: "Koro, the Creator, sent word to our forefathers long ages ago that he has already sent his Son into the world to accomplish something wonderful for all mankind. Later, however, our forefathers turned away from the truth about Koro's Son."

• The following civilizations all passed down stories about a lost book that would help them if it were ever rediscovered: the **Kachin** of northern Burma; the **Lahu** near Thailand and Laos; the **Wa** between Burma and Yunnan, China; the **Kui** of Thailand and Burma; the **Lisu** of China; and the **Karen** of Burma.

THINK ABOUT IT

"I believe in Christianity as I believe that the sun has risen: not only because I see it, but because by it I see everything else."

—C. S. Lewis

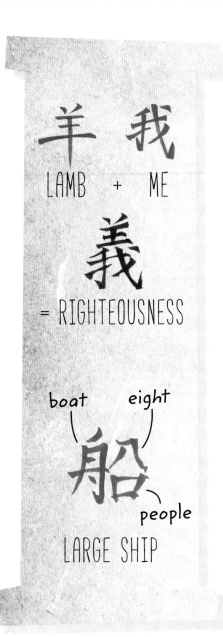

羊 我

LAMB + ME

義

= RIGHTEOUSNESS

boat   eight

船

people

LARGE SHIP

One fascinating example occurred in 1795, when one man from the Karen tribe described their lost book this way: "They say the author is *Y'wa*—the Supreme God."

• Once a year, the **Dyak** people of Borneo ceremonially place *Dosaku* ("my sin") on a boat containing a lantern and chicken, then they send the boat downriver, away from the village. As the boat floats out of sight, the villagers cry out, "*Selamat! Selamat!*" ["We're safe! We're safe!"].

• The written **Chinese** language contains over 200 basic symbols that are combined to form words or "characters." The Chinese character that means "righteousness" is comprised of the symbol for "lamb" written above the symbol for the word "me." How similar to the Bible's truth that people who take shelter under the sacrifice of the Lamb of God are considered righteous by God!

• The **Chinese** character for "large ship" contains the symbols for a boat, people, and the number eight (the very number of people who had taken refuge inside Noah's ark).

MORE TO EXPLORE ▶ If you'd like to get more answers to your questions about Christianity, you may want to read *The Case for Faith for Kids* by Lee Strobel with Robert Suggs and Robert Elmer.

34

SONGS FOR THE HEART

FOR THE LORD YOUR GOD . . . WILL TAKE DELIGHT IN YOU WITH GLADNESS. . . . HE WILL REJOICE OVER YOU WITH JOYFUL SONGS. ZEPHANIAH 3:17B NLT

God sings! And he wants us to sing, too. Did you know that songs and poetry fill about one-third of the Old Testament! Why is this? Because God wants us to love and worship him with our whole heart.

The word "psalm" means "song of praise." Let's look at how the Psalms help us worship.

1. The Psalms help us express our emotions. There are psalms of praise and thanksgiving for celebrating good times (Psalm 98, for example). There are psalms of lament to sing when we are sad (like Psalm 13). The Psalms help us express all kinds of emotion: grief (31:9), despair (69:20), joy (16:11),

PSALMS OF PRAISE

These psalms celebrate who God is, what he's like, and what he's done.

Examples:

Psalm 33, 100, 111, 113, 114, 117, 145, 146, 147, 150

PSALMS OF THANKSGIVING

These psalms celebrate specific ways God has taken action to help his people.

Examples:

Psalm 18, 21, 30, 32, 34, 92, 103, 107, 116, 118, 124, 138

PSALMS OF LAMENT

These psalms bring our sorrows and troubles before God—our grief, guilt, despair, enemies, etc.

Examples:

Psalm 3, 6, 7, 9, 12, 13, 25, 32, 38, 44, 51, 52, 55, 56, 57, 58, 62, 69, 70, 86, 89, 102, 120, 137, 140, 141, 143

What is the middle chapter in the entire Bible?
Psalm 118

What is the shortest chapter in the Bible?
Psalm 117 (2 verses)

What is the longest chapter in the Bible?
Psalm 119 (176 verses!)

loneliness (29:16), shame (69:19), awe (33:8), gladness (32:11), fear (23:4), and longing (38:9). The Psalms also remind us that we're not the first person to feel this way.

2. The Psalms remind us about God himself.

Whether life is sad or glad, God is always with us. The Psalms make this clear again and again. Throughout the Psalms (even in psalms of lament), God is regularly doing something good for his children. So, look for God in the Psalms: Where is he? What is he doing? How is he doing it? What has he promised? What is he like? What is he speaking? Why can you depend on him?

3. The Psalms help us praise God.

The Psalms give us words to say and sing to God. God wants us to engage with him with all our heart! You can start with a simple, "I love you," but there is so much more to say to God! If you were starting a fire, those words would be the fire starter. God gave us poetry and songs to add even more wood to the fire of our praise. Reading the Psalms is like stacking the fireplace of your heart with crisp, dry wood, which he will ignite into flames of worship!

THINK ABOUT IT

The poetry of the Psalms is "a gift from God that allows us to express our deepest heart responses to God and his truth in meaningful and memorable ways. It is a case of our hearts joining with our minds to say, 'Yes! Yes! Yes!' to the truths we are embracing."
—James Montgomery Boice

35

SEEING STARS

HE COUNTS THE STARS AND CALLS THEM ALL BY NAME.

PSALM 147:4 NLT

If you're hoping to read about movie stars, you've turned to the wrong chapter (wrong book, too). But the Bible does mention a certain kind of star: the ones you see in the night sky.

In Bible times, people used stars and constellations much more than most people do today. For one thing, with no bright city lights or pollution back then, stars could be seen more clearly than they are today. In Bible times stars were used to keep track of the days and seasons. Think about it: what would you do without a calendar or phone app to tell you the date? Stars were also used to navigate. There were no printed maps, but travelers knew which way to go by looking at the positions of the stars. (Verses to read: Genesis 1:14–16; Matthew 2:9; Acts 27:20)

The Bible mentions several constellations and stars.

Capella

Pleiades

Aldebáran

PLEIADES (THE SEVEN SISTERS)

The Pleiades is a tight cluster of stars in the
constellation Taurus. In the northern hemisphere,
first look for the constellation Auriga (shaped like a
pentagon). The brightest star in Auriga is Capella (a
bright yellow star). In November, Capella rises a few
hours after sunset. Look to the south of Capella for
a bright reddish-orange star, Aldebaran. The Pleiades
should be west-northwest of Aldebaran. (Pleiades is
mentioned in Job 9:9 and 38:31; and in Amos 5:8.)

More on next page ⟶

Polaris

Big Dipper

Ursa Major

Orion

Sirus

Canis Major

URSA MAJOR (THE BEAR)

Ursa Major, contains the well-known asterism (group of stars) known as the "Big Dipper." The handle of the dipper forms the "tail" of the bear. (Read Job 9:9 and 38:32.)

ORION (THE HUNTER)

In the winter, find Orion by looking toward the eastern horizon in December after 8 p.m. In the summer, Orion rises just before dawn in August. Orion's "belt" is comprised of three bright stars lined up in a row. (Orion is mentioned in Job 9:9 and 38:31; and in Amos 5:8.)

THE MAZZAROTH

The Bible also mentions an unknown constellation called The Mazzaroth, which is possibly Canis Major—the constellation that contains Sirius, the Dog Star (read Job 38:32). To find Sirius, look for the brightest star in the sky. The three stars of Orion's "belt" point to this bluish-white star.

Did You KNOW?

STAR OF WONDER

"Where is he who has been born king of the Jews? For we saw his star when it rose and have come to worship him." Matthew 2:2

For almost 2,000 years people have wondered what exactly was the "star" that led the wise men to Bethlehem. Was it a brand-new star that just appeared one night? But how could a star actually lead people? More than that, how could a star identify one particular house among many others in the village of Bethlehem? (Think about it—would you ever give directions to where you live by explaining that you—but not your neighbor—lived beneath a particular star?)

In 2015 Colin Nicholl, a Bible scholar, working with astronomers, announced a simply stellar discovery—which fits both the Bible and astronomy. Nicholl says that the "Star of Bethlehem" was most likely a large comet (which were commonly called "stars" back then—like we still call meteors "shooting stars" today).

If you'd like to learn more, you can read about it online or in Colin Nicholl's book, *The Great Christ Comet.*

TO EAT OR NOT TO EAT?

God made food and he made it to do more than fill your empty stomach. He could have made food with only one shape, color, and taste. Can you imagine plain, brown oatmeal for breakfast, lunch, and dinner—every day of your entire life?

But God created food with a wide variety of flavors, colors, and textures—not merely to eat, but to enjoy (1 Timothy 6:17).

Jesus enjoyed eating meals with others (Luke 7:34). If you had lived in Bible times, you would usually have eaten two meals a day, a smaller meal in the morning and a bigger one in the evening. Ruth 2:14 and 2 Samuel 25:18 give glimpses into ancient menus.

Clean or Unclean?

The Old Testament gave lots of rules about what you could eat. For example, the book of Exodus taught that meat and dairy could not be eaten together. Also foods were divided into two groups: "clean" food was OK to eat; "unclean" food was not OK to eat. Sadly, bacon and all pork were off the menu. You also could

DAILY FOOD ORDER

How much food did Solomon's palace use every day?

Answer: 180 bushels of flour, 360 bushels of grain, and 30 cows, 100 sheep or goats, plus deer, gazelles, and poultry (1 Kings 4:22)

SHOPPING LIST

Here are some foods that might have been on your dinner table had you lived in Bible times.

FRUITS AND VEGGIES

Apples (Song of Solomon 2:5)
Beans (2 Samuel 17:28)
Cucumbers (Isaiah 1:8)
Dates (1 Chronicles 16:3 NIV)
Figs (Nehemiah 13:15)
Grape Juice (Numbers 6:3)
Grapes (Matthew 7:16)
Leeks (Numbers 11:5)
Lentils (Genesis 25:34)
Melons (Numbers 11:5)
Olives (Deuteronomy 24:20)
Onions (Numbers 11:5)
Pomegranates
   (Deuteronomy 8.8)
Raisins (1 Samuel 25:18)

MEAT

Beef (Genesis 32:15)
Deer (Deuteronomy 14:5)
Dove (Leviticus 12:8)
Fish (Luke 24:42)
Goat (Genesis 27:9)
Lamb (2 Samuel 12:4)
Locust (Mark 1:6)
Oxen (1 Kings 19:21)
Partridge (1 Samuel 26:20)
Pigeon (Leviticus 12:8)
Quail (Psalm 105:40)
Sheep (Deuteronomy 14:4)
Veal (Luke 15:23)

BREADS, GRAINS AND NUTS

Almonds (Genesis 43:11)
Barley (Deuteronomy 8:8)
Bread (Mark 8:14)
Flour (1 Kings 17:12)
Millet (Ezekiel 4:9)
Pistachios (Genesis 43:11)
Roasted grain (Ruth 2:14)
Spelt (Ezekiel 4:9)
Unleavened Bread
   (Exodus 12:20)
Wheat (Deuteronomy 8:8)

DAIRY ITEMS

Butter (Job 29:6)
Cheese (1 Samuel 17:18)
Curds (cottage cheese) (Isaiah
   7:15)
Eggs (Luke 11:12)
Milk (Judges 5:25)

MISC

Cinnamon (Exodus 30:23)
Coriander seed
   (Exodus 16:31)
Cumin (Matthew 23:23)
Dill (Matthew 23:23)
Garlic (Numbers 11:5)
Honey (Genesis 43:11)
Mint (Matthew 23:23)
Mustard (Matthew 13:31)
Olive oil (Ezra 6:9;
   Deuteronomy 8:8)
Salt (Ezra 6:9)
Vinegar (Ruth 2:14)

Soft Flatbread

In Bible times, at Passover, bread was made without yeast—it was unleavened. Here's a recipe to make your own unleavened flatbread.

RECIPE

Soft Flatbread

Makes 4 flatbreads

Ingredients:

2 cups plain flour

1/2 teaspoon salt

3 ½ tablespoons butter

3/4 cups milk

1 tbsp olive oil (for greasing the frying pan)

What to do:

1. Put butter and milk into a small pan and heat until the butter is just melted (use a stove or microwave oven).

2. Measure flour into a medium-sized bowl. To measure, spoon flour lightly into a measuring cup [don't pack it down] and level the top.

3. Stir salt into flour.

4. Stir butter/milk mixture into the flour/salt until soft dough forms.

5. Knead the dough for a few minutes until it is smooth. Add a little extra flour if the dough is too sticky.

6. Wrap the ball of dough in plastic wrap and let it rest at room temperature for about 30 minutes.

7. Lightly flour the countertop or a cutting board. Unwrap the dough and divide it into 4 equal pieces. Roll each piece into a ball and then roll out each ball into a flat ¼-inch thick round.

8. Lightly oil a pan and place it on the stove over medium heat.

9. Place one flatbread in the pan, cook for about 1 minute until it bubbles up. Then flip and cook the other side.

10. Continue with remaining pieces of dough.

not eat shellfish, like shrimp and crabs (which sound delicious), or pests, like mice, bats, and moles (which don't). (You can read the details in Leviticus 11 and Deuteronomy 14.)

God had good reasons for all these rules. Israel was his people (Leviticus 11:45). They were supposed to reflect God's holiness (2 Samuel 7:23). He wanted his people to be clearly different than the pagan nations around them—even in the things they ate or didn't eat. He wanted to teach his people that becoming truly

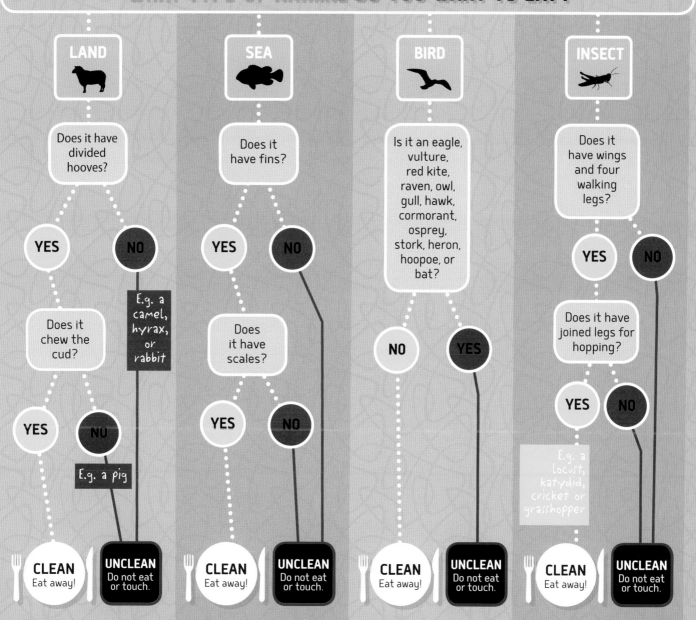

THINK
ABOUT IT

What is God's holiness?

When the Bible says something is "holy," it means that it is different from everything else. It is set apart or unique. So, for example, the priests used special vessels or pots and pans in their work around the temple. These weren't ordinary pots and pans that they could use at home. They were in a special category: for temple-use only. They were "holy" (1 Chronicles 22:19).

Yet more than anything else, God himself is holy. He is in a class by himself. There is no one like him. He is special, unique. There is only one God—and it is him! (And when God reveals his holiness, we see his glory: his God-ness on display.)

"clean" was something that only happened as you came to God for help. In the Old Testament God's people came to him with sacrifices. In the New Testament, Jesus is our sacrifice, and when we turn to him in faith, he makes us clean from the inside out.

And when Jesus came, he also changed all those Old Testament laws about food. He taught that now all food was considered clean. Jesus wanted us to know that what really made people unclean (sinful) wasn't the food that went into their stomachs, but the evil that came out of their hearts. (Verses to read: Matthew 15:10–20; Acts 10:9–15)

Now, it might turn your stomach to imagine digging into some roasted mole with a side order of deep fried bat! But that's how our sin-soaked thoughts, words, and actions make God feel. Sick! Yet Jesus took even those awful sins of his people on himself, carried them to the cross, and died for them. (Verses to read: Isaiah 53:4-6; 2 Corinthians 5:21)

Now as a result, all food is considered clean. And if you are one of God's children, you are too. Even when you sin, God isn't sick of you. He delights in you, because you belong to his perfect Son—the One he has always loved. (Verses to read: Matthew 3:17; John 13:10; 17:24)

MORE MEN WHO GAVE THEIR LIVES FOR CHRIST

JOHN HUSS

John Huss (also spelled *Jan Hus*) was born around 1369 and died in 1415. He grew up in a poor family in southern Bohemia (now the Czech Republic). John did not like being poor and decided to become a priest—mostly for the wealth and important friends it would bring him. He went to school in Prague, where eventually he became the preacher at Prague's Bethlehem Chapel. It was a large, very popular church. Somewhere along the way God opened John's heart to believe the gospel.

As a Christian, John now began to understand the Scriptures: "Desiring to hold, believe, and assert whatever is contained in them as long as I have breath in me." And his life changed. John began living a simple life, not caring about getting

"Therefore, faithful Christian, seek the truth, hear the truth, learn the truth, love the truth, speak the truth, adhere to the truth, defend the truth to death; for truth will make you free from sin, the devil, the death of the soul, and finally from eternal death."

rich. He even began preaching against other church leaders who were more interested in getting money for themselves than telling people about Jesus. When these church leaders told John to stop preaching against their sins, he refused.

So in 1414 the church leaders invited John to a meeting to talk things over. They promised Huss that he would be safe. They lied. When John arrived at the meeting, he was thrown into jail and falsely condemned. They said he was preaching "heresy" (teaching things that aren't in the Bible).

On July 6, 1415, John Huss, though innocent, was declared guilty. Before being burned alive, John said to his persecutors:

"Alas, drag my poor carcass to death so that you cannot sin any longer against an innocent victim! . . . My trust is in the Almighty God and in my Lord Jesus Christ, who has redeemed me and called me to preach his gospel to the last breath of life. . . . His blessed name be praised by all!"

Although Huss died that day, his example lived on. For the next 100 years, his death gave many believers courage to stand up for what was right, even though it might cost them their own lives. One of those Christians was a young man named Martin Luther.

MARTIN LUTHER

Martin Luther lived in Germany from 1483 to 1546. In those days Bibles were rare, so for years Martin could not read one for himself. The things he was taught about God were not true and comforting. Instead, his young mind was filled with false and terrifying thoughts of what God was like. Martin believed that God was a harsh Judge who would likely punish him forever. (This also fits Martin's life at home; his parents were so strict that he once was beaten for stealing a nut.)

When he grew up, Martin thought the way to make God like him more was to be more religious. So he became a monk and went to live in a monastery. He thought that harsh discipline was what God wanted from him. So he prayed more and ate less. He volunteered for the hardest jobs, like scrubbing the stone floors. He spent countless hours studying God's Word. But still he had no peace in his heart; he had no assurance that God loved him.

Then one day, he read this in Romans:

"Whatever your heart clings to and confides in, that is really your God."

"We are saved by faith alone, but the faith that saves is never alone."

149

THINK
ABOUT IT

FAITH AND WORKS

INCORRECT:
Salvation = Faith + Good Works

CORRECT:
Salvation + Faith = Good Works

For in [the gospel] the righteousness of God is revealed from faith for faith, as it is written, "the righteous shall live by faith." (Romans 1:17)

And God opened Martin's heart to understand the Good News that salvation comes through trusting Jesus, not by a person's own efforts. He saw that, because of Christ, God was not angry with him. Instead, through Christ Jesus, God declares all believers 100 percent "righteous." Of that moment Luther wrote, "I felt myself to have been reborn and to have gone through open doors into Paradise!"

Yet Martin's struggles were not over. As he began preaching that people could be saved by faith alone in Christ alone, many church leaders objected to what he taught. They thought that a person needed faith *plus* good works in order to please God and get into heaven. So, just as had happened to John Huss, the church leaders invited Martin Luther to a meeting and promised him that he would be safe. Martin's friends remembered what had happened to Huss (who's name means "goose"). His friends warned, "They'll cook **your** goose!"

But Luther trusted God and, in 1521, he went to the city called Worms (which in German means a "town in a watery area," not a bunch of wriggling earthworms) where he was called to defend what he had written. The church leaders asked,

"Martin, how can you assume that you are the only one to understand the sense of Scripture? Would you put your judgment above that of so many famous men and claim that you know more than they all? . . . Martin, answer candidly—do you or do you not repudiate [disown] your books and the errors which they contain?"

Luther replied,

"Unless I am convicted by Scripture and plain reason. . . . My conscience is captive to the Word of God. I cannot and will not recant anything, for to go against the conscience is neither right nor safe. God help me. Amen."

The church leaders condemned Luther, and on his journey home, Martin was kidnapped—by some friends—who took him secretly to Wartburg Castle, where he was placed in hiding for almost a year. During that time, Martin translated the entire New Testament into the common German language of his day. Now finally all the people could read the Good News of God's Word for themselves.

Martin would live for another 25 years. And during that time, he helped thousands more people hear and trust the Good News about Jesus Christ. He married when he was in his forties and, with his wife, raised six children. He preached several times a week and wrote several dozen hymns and many books. (His writings occupy 55 volumes!) Near the end of his life Martin Luther explained his success this way: "I did nothing. The Word did it all."

JOHN BUNYAN

John Bunyan (1628–1688) grew up near Bedford, England—over 80 years after and 700 miles distant from Martin Luther. As a child, John knew about the Bible, but he wasn't a Christian. John later wrote: "I had but few equals for cursing, swearing, lying, and blaspheming the holy name of God." During this part of his life, John was almost killed several times. One evening when John was in the army and scheduled for guard duty, a friend asked to take his place. That evening his friend was shot and killed. God had other plans for John.

Over time, Bunyan, along with Huss and Luther before him, came to see that Jesus had already lived a perfect life for them and died for all their sins. John wrote:

> [God] did cast into my hand a book of Martin Luther; it was his commentary on the book of Galatians . . . . I found my condition in his experience, so largely and profoundly handled, as if his book had been written out of my own heart. . . . I do prefer this book of Martin Luther on the Galatians, excepting the Holy Bible, before all books that ever I have seen.

"Pray often, for prayer is a shield to the soul, a sacrifice to God, and a scourge for Satan."

"If you have sinned, do not lie down without repentance; for the want of repentance after one has sinned makes the heart yet harder and harder."

John (and Martin) learned that a person's goodness or kindness didn't earn anything with God; Christ himself was "our righteousness" (our goodness). And as this Good News changed John's heart, it also began to move his mouth. Although he was only a poor tinker (someone who repairs pots and pans), John began preaching the Good News about Jesus to anyone who would listen. And *lots* of people did—Bunyan was an excellent preacher!

But England had an official state church that did not allow just anyone to preach. So John was taken away from his family and thrown into jail. He was told that he would be released if he promised to stop preaching about Jesus. Instead, John remained both faithful and imprisoned.

Life in jail was hard. It was crowded and there was little food. Yet he stood firm, saying: "If I was out of prison today, I would preach the gospel again tomorrow by the help of God." He declared, "I will stay in prison till the moss grows on my eye lids rather than disobey God."

Over his lifetime, John spent twelve years in prison. Yet while in his cell, John wrote one of the most famous books ever written in the English language: *The Pilgrim's Progress* (see page 116 for more details). It's been in print for over 300 years, translated into over 200 languages, and read by millions of people.

The servants of God may end up in chains, but the message of God can never be bound.

MORE TO
EXPLORE If you'd like to learn more about other godly people of the past, you may want to read, from the series, "Christian Biographies for Young Readers": *John Owen* by Simonetta Carr and Matt Abraxas; and *Jonathan Edwards* by Simonetta Carr.

38

PARENTS AREN'T PERFECT

I know this will come as a shock to you, but news flash: *your mom and dad make mistakes.*

They can lose their temper. They might not spend enough time with you. They probably don't let you do what you want. And they definitely will say embarrassing things. And that's just before breakfast.

How do you live with parents like this?

1. Remember that your parents are sinners (just like you). Hopefully they are trying their best to do what is right, but they sin like you do. No parent has all the answers, understands every detail, and responds in the perfect way. Your mom and dad are your parents, but don't forget: they are also limited human beings who struggle with sin and need the Savior, just like you do. (Verses to read: Ephesians 6:4; Colossians 3:21)

2. **Trust that God put you in the perfect family.** Perfect for you, that is. This doesn't mean that your family is perfect. But when God placed you in your family, he knew exactly what he was doing. You fit. He arranges families for your good. You have the mom and dad you do (even if they're not your biological mom or dad) because God did it. Because your parents are sinners, they will disappoint you. But you can be confident (even if your family is driving you crazy right now) that one day you will be able to see God's good plan for your family. (Verses to read: Romans 8:28; Genesis 50:20)

3. **Get help if you are in danger.** It's awful to think about, but some children have been physically hurt by grown-ups. Sometimes even family members do evil things against children. If you are in physical danger or have been hurt like this, please talk to a grown-up you can trust. Some safe people to talk with could be a teacher, a school counselor, a doctor, or a pastor. The Lord will help you. (Verse to read: Psalm 27:10)

4. **Let sinful parents point you to the perfect Parent.** Your dad is your father. But God is *THE* Father—the ultimate Father. Before he even created the world, he has always been Father. Being Father is not just something God does. It is who he is. God IS Father in all he does. This means that the whole concept of fathers (and mothers) comes from God. So let your parents—even in their flaws—point you to the Father who will always protect and provide for you. (Verses to read: John 17:24; Ephesians 3:14–15)

39

NIGHT AND DAY DIFFERENCES

DAY

BIBLE TIME

NIGHT

Noon

Sunrise

Sunset

Midnight

Have you ever wondered what the Bible means when it mentions odd-sounding times of day like these?

"about the third hour"
(Matthew 20:3)

"at the seventh hour"
(John 4:52)

"in the second watch"
(Luke 12:38)

Here's how people kept track of time back then. Daytime was divided into 12 equal parts or "hours." The first hour started at sunrise. The last ended at sunset. (And, yes, this means that "hours" were different lengths depending on the length of the day. In the winter the hours were shorter than in the summer.)

Nights worked the same way. Night was divided into 12 equal parts or "hours." There were 12 hours of night, with midnight ending the sixth hour of the night and sunrise ending the twelfth hour. These night hours were divided into several blocks or "watches," during which a guard might stand watch. The Jewish people divided the night into three watches, the Romans into four.

THINK ABOUT IT

WHAT [BIBLE] TIME IS IT?

To figure out approximately what Bible time it is, look at your clock:

- If it's before lunch, subtract 6 from the hour on your clock.

- If it's after lunch, add 6 to the hour on your clock.

- If it's after supper, subtract 6 from the hour on your clock.

- If it's after midnight, add 6 to the hour on your clock.

For example: If your clock says 10 a.m., subtract 6. In Bible time, then, it is the 4th hour.

Problem: Your clock says 5 p.m. What time is it in Bible time?

Problem: Your clock says 9 pm. What time is it in Bible time?

Answer: 5 p.m. + 6 = 11th hour of the day in Bible time

Answer: 9 p.m. − 6 = 3rd hour of the night in Bible time

Who are the four oldest people in the Bible?

40

HOW TO GLIMPSE GOD

For ever since the world was created, people have seen the earth and sky. Through everything God made, they can clearly see his invisible qualities—his eternal power and divine nature. So they have no excuse for not knowing God.

Romans 1:19–20 NLT

Have you ever noticed how windows fog up on rainy days? You can look out and see only shapes of trees, houses, and cars.

The Bible says that we see God in the same way (1 Corinthians 13:12). Of course, no human on the planet can actually look at God with his own eyes. But God created this world to be like a foggy window through which you can catch glimpses of what he is like (Psalm 19:1).

But the question is: *how* can we glimpse God in the world he has made?

Read the Scripture verses to discover examples of where in creation you might learn about God. Then look at the photos and think about what they show about our Creator God.

Martin Luther said that we see God "partly through his works, mainly through his Word." In creation we can see what God is like through looking at what he has made, but in the Bible we see an even clearer picture of God. And this biblical picture of God is clearest when we look at Jesus Christ. If you want to know what God is like, take a long look at Jesus. When you read Matthew, Mark, Luke, or John, don't start with ideas of what God is like, and then try to find ways that Jesus matches that kind of God. Instead, begin by looking at and listening to Jesus. He will show you exactly and perfectly what God is like. (Verses to read: Hebrews 1:1–4)

▶ JOB 36:24-33   JOB 37:5-12   PSALM 8:1-4   PSALM 19:1-6   PSALM 29:3-11   JEREMIAH 5:22

JEREMIAH 31:35   ACTS 14:15-17   ACTS 17:26-28   ROMANS 1:20   ROMANS 2:14-16

Answers: Job 36:24–33 (thunderstorms); Job 37:5–12 (winter storms); Psalm 8:1–4 (outer space, moon, stars); Psalm 19:1–6 (sky, outer space); Psalm 29:3–11 (winds); Jeremiah 5:22 (seashore); Jeremiah 31:35 (regular schedule of sun, moon, stars, and oceans); Acts 14:15–17 (rain, seasons, harvests); Acts 17:26–28 (nations); Romans 1:20 (general blessings of creation); Romans 2:14–16 (conscience).

41

HOW TO PROFIT FROM THE PROPHETS

Parents: "Please go tell your brother to stop playing, come inside, and clean his room."

You: "Mom wants you to clean your room."

Brother: (keeps on playing)

You: "Hey, Mom said come inside and clean!"

Brother: "What'd you say?"

You: "MOM SAID GET IN HERE RIGHT NOW!"

The prophets could have told you: It's not easy being this kind of messenger. God had made Israel his people and given them his Law. Yet like the brother who wants to keep on playing, lots of times God's people didn't want to listen to God or his messengers, the prophets. Israel wanted to do what *they* wanted to do. Here are some other ways to understand the job of the Old Testament prophets . . .

The prophets were like referees.

The prophets acted like modern-day *referees*, blowing the whistle when God's people, rejecting God's Law, went out of bounds. They tried to help God's people listen and follow God. Some prophets even preached against wicked kings, who had the power to execute them. (And some did!)

But God didn't give up on his people. In the Old Testament, he kept sending his messengers—lots of them. Thankfully, they also brought good news.

The prophets were like sports announcers.

The prophets didn't just warn God's people. They also promised that God would one day bless his people. In this way, the prophets acted like *sports announcers* predicting how things would turn out. They spoke encouraging messages to God's sinful people: "The LORD still loves you. Turn away from your sin. He promises that one day he will send the perfect Savior and King to wash away your sin and set everything right again." Sin had brought ruin, said the prophets, but there was hope for tomorrow. Their basic message seems simple, but many people still find the prophets difficult to read.

The prophets were like coaches.

Have you ever watched a ball game and seen a coach signaling to the players? Sometimes they'll communicate the next play by shouting a secret code name or making a strange sign with their hands. The coach knows what he's communicating, and the players know what he's

1/3 PROPHECY

About one-third of the Bible is classified as "prophecy," with about 18 of its 66 books devoted mostly to prophecy. There were "writing" prophets and "speaking" prophets. The writing prophets wrote down their messages in the books of the Bible called the major and minor prophets ("major" because they're longer, "minor" because they're shorter). These prophets include Isaiah, Jeremiah, Ezekiel, Daniel, Hosea, Amos, and others.

communicating. But the fans and (hopefully) the other team's players don't. Why? Because the coach and players have spent a lot of time together—they've planned and talked and practiced. The signs and codes are familiar to them. It's the same with the prophets.

If you've ever read from one of the prophetic books of the Bible, you'll know it's not easy to understand. But the prophets knew God's message and the people of God knew too. Why? Because they lived at the same time period, in the same area, and experienced lots of the same things. So, when you read the prophets, always keep in mind that to understand what's written, you'll need to learn more about what was going on back then. This is where books, study Bibles, and your pastors or teachers can be a real help to you.

𝄞 𝄞 𝄞

Reading the prophets isn't easy. But here are some basic practice exercises to get you started.

Which Old Testament book is quoted most in the New Testament?
Answer: Isaiah (419 times); Psalms is second with 414 quotes

162

Read the following passages and then ask yourself the follow-up questions below.

Isaiah 1:1–20 & 30:15
Jeremiah 18:1–11 & 29:13
Hosea 14:1–7
Amos 5:4–15
Micah 6:1–8

when you read the prophets, ask...

> 1st

Am I disobeying God? What needs to change in my life?

> 2nd

Where in the prophecy does God promise grace, mercy, blessing, forgiveness, or a Savior? What do you learn about God's heart towards his sinful people? What has God promised to do for me because I belong to Jesus?

> 3rd

Are there any details in this passage that I don't understand? Are there any names or places or events that I can investigate more?

42

DESIGNER GENES (AND MORE)

THE HEAVENS DECLARE THE GLORY OF GOD, AND THE SKY ABOVE PROCLAIMS HIS HANDIWORK.

PSALM 19:1

Science and mathematics may (or may not) be your favorite subjects. But whether you like them or not, they both give evidence that God is real. No one can scientifically "prove" that God exists. But what better explanation is there for the facts below?

SIMPLE COMPLEXITY

Your body is made up of trillions of cells. Every cell that has a nucleus contains DNA. DNA is like a recipe—it's the material that holds all the information (called "genes") about how you look and how the parts of your body work. It determines your gender; your eye color; your hair color; the shape of your earlobe, chin, and hairline; and whether you have dimples—just to name a few.

Interestingly, about 99.9 percent of the DNA of every human on earth is exactly the same. It's that other one-tenth of one percent that makes everyone different from everyone else.

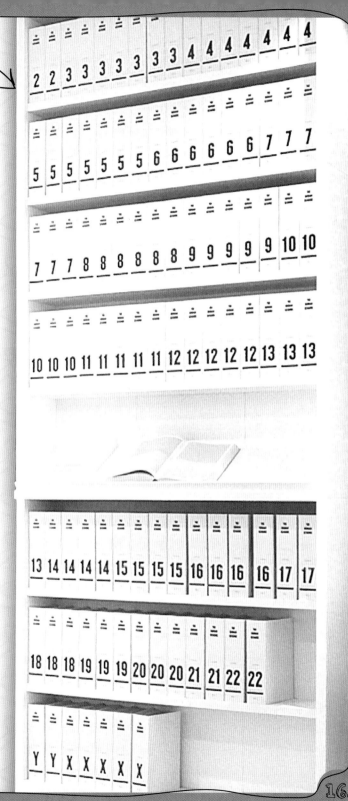

Actual bookcase of DNA info for the cell of ONE human genome

But what's even more amazing is that your DNA recipe (also called a "genome") contains more than 3 billion building blocks of information (called "base pairs").

This much information is about equal to three gigabytes of computer data storage—again, all contained within one cell. That's like having 200 books, each 1,000 pages long, inside one tiny cell. It would take someone over nine years to read that much information!

Little did you suspect when you got ready this morning that you put clothing over 15 quintillion (15,000,000,000,000,000,000) "pages" of information. (Just think how cool it'd be if you could tap into that kind of information when taking a test at school.)

How do you explain the existence of all this information? Truly there must be a God who created each one of us. We are "fearfully and wonderfully made" (Psalm 139:14) by a mighty and wise Creator.

PREDICTABLE PATTERNS

God made a universe that runs on

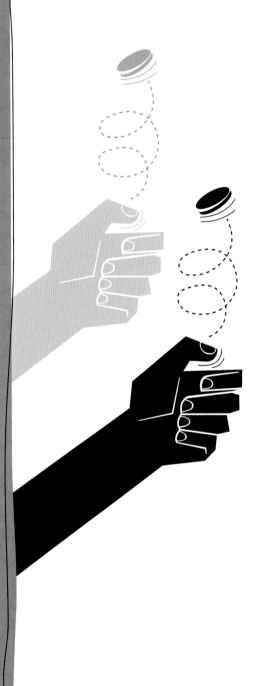

patterns you can depend on. Here is an example:

Dr. Theodore P. Hill asks his mathematics students at the Georgia Institute of Technology to go home and either (A) flip a coin 200 times and write down the results, or (B) merely *pretend* to flip a coin and write down 200 fake results. The following day, to the astonishment of the students, the teacher, just by glancing at the homework can tell who has faked their tosses.

What the students usually don't know is that the odds are overwhelming that they will throw at least six heads or six tails in a row.

This dependability in nature has been called "Benford's Law," named after Dr. Frank Benford (1883–1948). This law states that so-called random numbers aren't really random, but exist in predictable patterns. There is no such thing as pure chance in our universe.

And there are other dependable laws that are more well known. If you jump off a cliff, you can count on it—gravity will be the last law you break. If you measure the speed of light, your results will always be 186,000 miles per second. If you wait twenty-four hours or so, the sun will be in about the same place in the sky.

God's world follows the patterns that God designed.

FINE-TUNED LAWS

Did you realize that gravity is a relatively *weak* force? Take a tiny magnet, and see how easily it overcomes gravity to lift paper clips from a table. Yet, if gravity is so comparatively weak, why do falls on an icy sidewalk hurt so much?

The answer is that the force of gravity working on an object doubles as that object's mass doubles. (In other words: the bigger you are, the harder you fall.) That's why creatures with less mass, mice for example, can fall for a distance several times their body length, yet not get hurt.

But if we imagined a universe with strong gravity, says scientist Martin Rees, "no animal could be much larger than insects, and even they would need thick legs to support them. Gravity would crush anything as large as ourselves. . . . Stars . . . would be so densely packed that close encounters [collisions] would be frequent. This would in itself preclude stable planetary systems, because the orbits would be disturbed by passing stars— something that (fortunately for our Earth) is unlikely to happen in our own Solar System."

The precise laws of gravity, which we need in order to live on our planet (Job 36:26), require an all-powerful, all-knowing Designer. It is God who holds all things together—whether atoms or galaxies (Colossians 1:17).

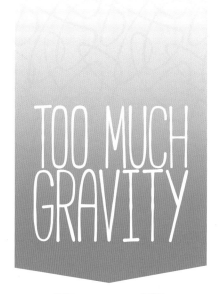

MORE TO EXPLORE ▶

If you'd like to learn more about God and nature, you may want to read *Case for a Creator for Kids* by Lee Strobel with Robert Suggs & Robert Elmer.

43

HOW TO PRAY

What do you pray for? It's easy to just ask God for whatever you want.

"I really want a new iPad."

"I would like pink shoes to match my dress."

"Please give me a new brother. (The one I have is messed up.)"

But God also wants you to ask for important things that could change your life.

Thankfully, God has let us know the kind of things he wants us to pray for. You'll find a lot of them in the most well-known prayer in the Bible: "the Lord's Prayer." (It's called the Lord's Prayer, because the Lord Jesus gave this prayer as an example of how to pray.)

Our Father in heaven, hallowed be your name. Your kingdom come, your will be done, on earth as it is in heaven. Give us this day our daily bread, and forgive us our debts, as we also have forgiven our debtors. And lead us not into temptation, but deliver us from evil. Matthew 6:9–13

Here is a helpful way to think about this model prayer.

Have you ever been to summer camp? Most of the time, a week away from home is fun! New friends, crazy games, and candy overload! But sometimes, camp can be hard—like it must be for the camper who wrote this postcard:

Dear Mom and Dad,

I really miss you and wish you were here. I know that if you were here the food would be better for sure! And I bet so many kids wouldn't be sick! Could you please send a care package? I need snacks and warm clothes. All the rain has made the hiking trails slick and dangerous. One kid fell and had to be taken to the ER yesterday. One good thing: only a few days left. Please come early on Saturday—even better, come on Friday!

Love, Andre

The Lord's Prayer is a little bit like this postcard from camp: it is the cry of a heart that's homesick for God. The first two sentences of the Lord's Prayer plead with God to come and make this world right again. But since God has not yet made everything new, the last two sentences ask God to meet our needs on this fallen planet (for help, forgiveness, and protection).

THINK ABOUT IT

One day, while giving Martin Luther a haircut, his barber asked for some advice on how to pray. Here's what Luther later wrote to him:

"A good and attentive barber keeps his thoughts, attention, and eyes on the razor and hair and does not forget how far he has gotten with his shaving or cutting. If he wants to engage in too much conversation or let his mind wander or look somewhere else, he is likely to cut his customer's mouth, nose, or even his throat! Thus if anything is to be done well, it requires full attention of all one's senses and members. This in short is the way I use the Lord's Prayer, when I pray it."

MODELING THE LORD'S PRAYER

Pray your own prayer modeled after the one Jesus taught us.

1 OUR FATHER IN HEAVEN, HALLOWED BE YOUR NAME.

We pray that the whole world would know you are holy and worship you alone.

2 YOUR KINGDOM COME, YOUR WILL BE DONE, ON EARTH AS IT IS IN HEAVEN.

Set everything right; make all things in this world new again.

3 GIVE US THIS DAY OUR DAILY BREAD.

Give us what we need each day—food, clothing, shelter. We trust you to know exactly what we need.

4 AND FORGIVE US OUR DEBTS, AS WE ALSO HAVE FORGIVEN OUR DEBTORS.

Please forgive us for all the things we have done wrong—and then help us to also forgive those who have done wrong things to us.

5 AND LEAD US NOT INTO TEMPTATION, BUT DELIVER US FROM EVIL.

Help us to walk close to you, depending on you to protect us from sinning.

Did you know the Bible is packed with other prayers too? You can learn a lot about praying by thinking about those prayers. Here are some that are grouped into several categories.

LORD, MAKE YOURSELF FAMOUS

Hezekiah prayed, "Help us so the whole world will know that you are the one true God." (2 Kings 19:19)

Jeremiah prayed, "Forgive us so that your reputation for mercy will spread around the world." (Jeremiah 14:7)

Solomon and Habakkuk both prayed, "May your glory cover the dry land like the waters cover the sea." (Psalm 72:19; Habakkuk 2:14)

LORD, WE PRAISE YOU

David prayed, "God, I will bless you with all my heart." (Psalm 103:1)

Mary prayed, "My soul rejoices and magnifies you, Lord, because you have done great things for me." (Luke 1:46-50)

LORD, WE THANK YOU

Paul prayed, "Lord, thank you for making people I know more like Jesus." (2 Thessalonians 1:3)

Asaph prayed, "We thank you, God, because you are always near us." (Psalm 75:1)

LORD, FORGIVE ME

Daniel prayed, "We have ignored and disobeyed your Word, O Lord. Forgive us." (Daniel 9:5-6, 19)

Ezra prayed, "Forgive me; I am so ashamed of my sin; it's piled up like a mountain." (Ezra 9:6)

LORD, HELP OTHER PEOPLE

An unnamed woman prayed, "Jesus, please take care of my daughter's needs." (Matthew 15:22-28)

Paul prayed, "Help my friends love the people around them." (1 Thessalonians 3:12)

LORD, HELP ME

Hannah prayed, "O Lord, please remember me and have compassion on me." (1 Samuel 1:10-11)

Asa prayed, "Lord, there is no one else who can help me; I am relying on you alone." (2 Chronicles 14:11)

44

HARD WORK? NO SWEAT!

I leapt out of bed as the garbage truck rumbled down the street. I was twelve-years-old and had forgotten to do my weekly job—take out the trash! This wasn't the first time I'd forgotten and, as a result, trash had been piling up in the backyard. My dad had threatened, "If the trash doesn't go out this week, it will stay in your room until next week."

That's why I found myself chasing the garbage truck in my pajamas! I had to catch that truck! I knew what would happen to my room (and my sense of smell) if the trash didn't go out today.

But my problem wasn't just that I had forgotten. There was more: *I didn't like to work.* Over the years, the Lord had a lot to teach me about work and about himself. Here are a few things that I've learned.

1. God is a worker.

Because God works, we do too. After all, we have been made in his image. In the Bible God describes himself as many different kinds of workers: a potter (Isaiah 64:8), a tailor (Genesis 3:21), a farmer (Isaiah 5:1), a warrior (Habakkuk 3:10–15), a shepherd (Psalm 23:1–4), and a host (Psalm 23:5–6)! So, when we work to make things, we also reflect the one who made *us* from the dust of the ground. Artists use paint, clay, metal, etc. to make things. Musicians use sounds to create and play music. Writers, poets, reporters, and philosophers use words to give form to ideas and observations. Doctors use an array of materials to diagnose and treat sickness and injury. Chefs use meat, vegetables, fruit, herbs, spices, etc. to make delicious food. And the list goes on. Every human being has the capacity to make things because we are all made in the image of our God who works. (Verses to read: Genesis 1:1, 27)

2. God is a designer.

Where did work come from? You might think it started because of sin. Sometimes it feels like punishment! But actually, work is part of God's design in creation. God put Adam in the Garden of Eden with a to-do list. Work has been part of God's good design from the very beginning.

> # Whatever you do, work heartily, as for the Lord and not for men.
> ### colossians 3:23

It's because of sin that work became *difficult*. But God still expects you to work. So when you have to help fold clothes, mow the lawn, clean the bathroom, or sweep up a mess, remember that work—even though it may be hard, boring, or disgusting—is still part of God's design for your life. (Verses to read: Genesis 1:26; 2:15; 3:17–19)

3. God is a boss.

God also gives his children particular jobs. For example, he called Saul and David to be kings; Jeremiah and Ezekiel to be prophets; and Bezalel and Oholiab to be craftsmen and artists (Exodus 35:34–35).

But did you know that God is *your* boss? When you work on a job that your parents asked you to do—even everyday chores—who are you *really* working for? When you work "you are serving the Lord Christ" (Colossians 3:23, 34).

So don't follow my example. Chasing garbage trucks in your pajamas is not something I would recommend. Instead, learn to enjoy work—homework or helping around the house. Work hard out of love for the Lord.

How many workers cut stone for building Solomon's Temple?

Answer: 150,000 stone cutters (1 Kings 5:15; 2 Chronicles 2:18)

45

THE GREATEST ^Love STORY IN THE HISTORY OF THE WORLD

History-*His* story-is a love story. And the Bible tells us how it all began: with God. Genesis 1:1 says, "In the beginning, God created the heavens and the earth." But what was God doing *before* he created everything?

Love Is (before creation)

Jesus prays, "Father . . . you loved me even before the world began" (John 17:24). Before creation, God loved. God has always loved his Son. And the Son has always loved the Father. God the Father, God the Son, and God the Holy Spirit—the three members of the Godhead—have always loved each other. God was never alone and never lonely. This is why the apostle John writes, "God *is* love" (1 John 4:8). Loving is what God has always done. (Verse to read: John 14:31)

Love Shares (at creation)

God wanted to share his love with others. So, God created a world that displays his amazing love. He

created Adam and Eve, the first man and woman, to enjoy his love. They would feel his love as they enjoyed and took care of the wonderful world he had made. They would know his love as they filled the earth with children who loved God too. And in all this, they enjoyed and loved God most of all. So, in the beginning, for a time, everything was perfect. Nothing was wrong: there were no tears, no pain, no sickness, no sin, and at least for a little while, no homework. (Verses to read: 1 Timothy 6:17; Psalm 19:1–2; Genesis 2:16, 17, 28)

Love Rejected (in the garden)

But then Adam and Eve did something that had terrible consequences. They decided to live by their own rules instead of God's. Adam and Eve ate the fruit that God had told them not to eat. They chose to love something God had made more than they loved God himself. The Bible calls this "idolatry." God's love didn't change, but his perfect world was no longer perfect. (Verses to read: Genesis 3:1–7)

Love Continues (outside the garden)

Even after Adam and Eve rejected him, God continued to love them. God could easily have left them alone or destroyed them and started all over. Instead, he pursued them. God's love was unchanged, but because they had sinned, Adam and Eve could no longer enjoy God's love like they had before. He sent them out of the garden and told them that life would be much, much harder. And their relationship with their loving God was broken. But God promised that they would not live in a broken relationship with him forever.

In the years that followed, Adam and Eve's children started to fill the world. But life was hard, just as God said it would be. Sadly, most people didn't love God with all their hearts. And before long, the world was overflowing with sin and pain and hate. (Verses to read: Genesis 3:21–24; 6:5)

So God judged sin by flooding the entire world, cleaning away all but a sampling of each animal and the family of a man named Noah. However, even after the flood, it wasn't long before the earth again was filled with people who had rejected God as Lord and loved what he had made (*themselves!*) more than God himself. (Verses to read: Genesis 7:1–4; 9:20–21; 11:1–8)

Love Rescues (through Abraham)

But God's love never changed. God now chose one of these sinners to bring his loving rescue plan to the entire world. His name was Abram (later known as Abraham), and through Abraham's family all the other families of the world would be blessed by God's love and grace. Romans 4:3 reminds us, "Abraham believed God, and God counted him as righteous because of his faith." But Abraham and his family also continued to sin. (Verses to read: Genesis 12:1–3)

Love Provides (for Israel)

But Abraham and his children and grandchildren were God's people. God loved them. So he rescued them from starvation and slavery. He gave them food, water, clothes, and even promised them a beautiful land they could call home. But God's people (Israel) didn't love God best and didn't do a good job of displaying

How long were Noah and his family inside the ark?

Are we there yet?

Answer: Just over one year (Genesis 7:11; 8:14)

God's love to the world. In fact, the people of Israel either fell in love with the good things God gave them or else they complained about them instead. (Verses to read: Genesis 37–47; Exodus 1–15; Numbers 14)

Eventually, God sent enemies to take away what he had given his people. When this happened, Israel cried to God for help. God sent rescuers and life was good again. But it didn't last long. When a leader died, the people stopped loving God, and so God would send enemies once more. Sadly, the same thing happened again and again. (You can read about this in the book of Judges.) What God's people needed was a good leader that would last.

Eventually, God gave his people kings to rule them. But even the best ones (like David or Solomon) didn't love God with their whole heart. They too loved what God had made more than God himself. And Israel followed their leaders into sin. So much for displaying God to the whole world! (You can read about these kings in the books of 1 & 2 Samuel and 1 & 2 Kings.)

Love Pursues (through prophets)

Then God sent prophets to remind his people how much he still loved them. (See page 160 to learn more about the prophets.) The prophets said: "Stop loving the stuff God has made, more than God himself. God loves you and wants you to love him in return." But God's people didn't listen. So, God sent enemies who took his people out of their homeland and brought them to a foreign land.

Love Restores (from exile)

Far away from home, God's people cried to him for mercy. In his love, God eventually brought them back home. But by now their land had been taken over by wicked people who didn't know God's love at all. Instead of sharing God's love

Which Israelite king ruled the longest amount of time?
Answer: Manasseh: 55 years (2 Kings 21:1)

with the foreigners in their land, God's people decided they would keep God's love all to themselves. They also continued to sin in lots of other ways.

What would happen now? God's people needed a king who would rescue them—not just from enemies—but from *sin itself*! This true king would restore their love for God and help them display his love to the whole world.

Love Arrives (in Jesus's birth and life)

God sent his very own Son to the earth. His name was Jesus, a member of Abraham's family and a royal descendant of King David. His mother was Mary, but he didn't have an earthly father. His Father was the God of the universe! As the perfect King, Jesus always loved and obeyed God with all his heart. He was everything that God's people were created to be, yet because of sin never were.

Love Sacrifices (in Jesus's ministry and death)

Jesus displayed God's love. By his miracles, Jesus showed what a world fixed by love (a "new creation") would look like: one with no more death, pain, or sickness—one with no more sin. And when he died on the cross, Jesus rescued his people by taking all their sin on himself. On the cross, Jesus endured the pain and broken relationship with God that had come as a consequence of sin. God's sinless Son was sent away from his Father, so that we, God's sinful people, might be brought home to the Father forever.

Love Conquers (in Jesus's resurrection)

Then the most amazing thing happened! Jesus who was crucified, died, and was buried in a garden tomb, didn't stay in the grave. He was raised from the dead. Once again a Man stood in a garden, perfect. This new Man had succeeded where

His robes for mine: such anguish none can know.

Christ, God's beloved, condemned as though His foe.

He, as though I, accursed and left alone;

I, as though He, embraced and welcomed home!

— "His Robes for Mine" lyrics, Chris Anderson

the first one had failed. This new Adam had reversed the brokenness caused by the first Adam. Love defeated death! God the Father accepted Jesus's death for all who believe in him. Now all who put their faith in Jesus have eternal life.

Love Spreads (through the church)

Jesus's supreme display of love for sinners is Good News—it is the gospel! Before Jesus returned to his Father, he told his people to follow the same basic plan that God had given to Adam and Eve: Display and spread the news of God's love to the whole world. Fill the earth with people who, rescued from sin by Jesus, are now freed to love God more than anything else.

The rest of the New Testament (from Acts to Jude) shows how Jesus's people obeyed his plan. From the land of Israel to the headquarters of the known world (Rome), the followers of Jesus spread the message of God's love. But there was a problem.

Love Triumphs (in a restored creation)

Until God makes everything new at the end of time, the relationship between God and his people still needs work. Sadly God's people live in a sinful world, and they themselves still sin. They don't yet love God with all their heart. But one day, God will restore everything perfectly.

Jesus will come back again and fully remove all suffering, pain, and sin. He will completely transform his sinful people and this sinful world. And best of all, he will live with his people forever. On that day, everything will finally be as God created it to be. God's people will enjoy God's good world. Most of all, they will enjoy God himself.

And that brings us—not to the end. For when that day comes, it will only be the *beginning*.

MORE TO EXPLORE If you'd like to learn more about the story line of the Bible, you may want to read *God's Big Picture* by Vaughan Roberts.

46

BFF?
BEST FRIENDS FOREVER?

You may have 978 "friends" on social media, but what kind of friend are you in real life? The basics of being a friend aren't complicated: If you want a friend, be a friend.

But what is friendship all about?

Friendship Comes from God

God has always, through all eternity, been in relationship within the Trinity—God the Father, God the Son, and God the Holy Spirit have always been united as One. Since we're made in God's image, we have the same characteristic— that same quality. We, like God, want to be in relationship with others. That's how God designed us. God created Eve for Adam because "it is not good that the man should be alone" (Genesis 2:18).

Friendship Comes Naturally

The Bible talks about a close friend as someone "who is as your own soul" (Deuteronomy 13:6). David (yes, the David who killed Goliath) became best friends with King Saul's son, Jonathan. First Samuel 18:1 says, "The soul of Jonathan was knit to the soul of David." They got along great! They just clicked!

Friendships don't always form instantly the first time you meet someone, but friendships aren't rocket science either. Here are some first steps to remember about making friends:

1. Don't try to force someone to be a friend.

2. Pray that God would give you a friend who loves Jesus (2 Corinthians 7:6).

3. Enjoy the people around you. Stop trying to find a friend; instead, just be a friend.

4. Concentrate on making choices that please God (Proverbs 16:7).

5. Enjoy your friendship with God most of all (John 15:13; Romans 5:10).

THINK ABOUT IT

C. S. Lewis on Friendship

"Friendship is the greatest of worldly goods. Certainly to me it is the chief happiness of life. If I had to give a piece of advice to a young man about a place to live, I think I should say, 'sacrifice almost everything to live where you can be near your friends.'"

"Friendship must be about something, even if it were only an enthusiasm for dominoes or white mice. Those who have nothing can share nothing; those who are going nowhere can have no fellow-travellers."

WARNING!

The Bible warns us that we become like the people we hang out with (1 Corinthians 15:33). So be careful how you pick your friends.

The Lord reminds us to watch out for people who:

- **are angry** (Proverbs 22:24–25)
- **steal** (Proverbs 29:24)
- **reject God's ways** (Proverbs 14:7)
- **live in arrogance** (Proverbs 16:19)
- **stir up trouble** (Proverbs 24:1–2)
- **love to gossip** (Proverbs 20:19)

Friendship Comes with Responsibilities

So, you want to be a friend. What does a friend look like? What does a friend do? The Bible teaches that friends take responsibility to help each other:

1. A friend loves and serves—in good times and bad times (Proverbs 17:17; 18:24; 27:10).

2. A friend takes time with the other person and talks to them openly (Exodus 33:11; John 15:15).

3. A friend encourages the other person to be more like Jesus (Proverbs 27:5–6, 17).

4. A friend is not easily offended or hurt (Proverbs 10:12; 17:9).

5. A friend uses words to build up, not tear down or gossip about others (Proverbs 20:19; Ephesians 4:29).

What kind of friend are you?

47

THE LONG AND SHORT OF IT

If someone asked you what you believe, what would you say? Of course, Christians believe the Bible. But as you know, the Bible is a very *long* book, so it's a big help to have some way to *summarize* the Bible's truths.

A summary is like a sum in that it's a short version of something longer. For example, this list of six numbers can be added (summed) and written as one number:

$$1 + 2 + 3 + 4 + 5 + 6 = 21$$

When it comes to God's Word, why would you even want a shortened version of what the Bible teaches? First, a summary makes it easier to recall what is true. (Shorter is easier to remember than longer.) And secondly, a summary makes it easier to recognize what is false. (How could you detect what's wrong, if you don't have a firm grip on what's right?)

Did you know that the Bible itself gives us this kind of summary statement? Many of these biblical summaries take the truth of all four Gospels and squeeze them into just a few verses. Here are some of these summary passages from Scripture.

Now I would remind you, brothers, of the gospel I preached to you, which you received, in which you stand, and by which you are being saved, if you hold fast to the word I preached to you—unless you believed in vain. For I delivered to you as of first importance what I also received: that Christ died for our sins in accordance with the Scriptures, that he was buried, that he was raised on the third day in accordance with the Scriptures, and that he appeared to Cephas, then to the twelve. 1 Corinthians 15:1–5

*Great indeed, we confess, is the mystery of godliness: He was manifested in the flesh, vindicated by the Spirit, seen by angels, proclaimed among the nations, believed on in the world, taken up in glory.
1 Timothy 3:16*

Never forget that Jesus Christ was a man born into King David's family and that he was raised from the dead. This is the Good News I preach. 2 Timothy 2:8 NLT

About 130 years after the apostle Paul wrote these verses, Irenaeus, a pastor and missionary in what is now France, put together a summary of important Bible truths. He said that Christians believed:

In one God, the Father Almighty, who made the heaven and the earth and the seas and all the things that are in them; and in one Christ Jesus, the Son of God, who was made flesh for our salvation; and in the Holy Spirit, who made known through the prophets the plan of salvation, and the coming, and the birth from a virgin, and the passion [suffering and death], and the resurrection from the dead, and the bodily ascension into heaven of the beloved Jesus Christ, our Lord, and his future appearing from heaven in the glory of the Father to sum up all things and to raise anew all flesh of the whole human race.

By the fourth century, many Christians were summarizing what they believed by affirming a statement that later became known as "The Apostles' Creed." This creed is called the Apostles' Creed not because it was produced by the apostles themselves but because it contains a brief summary of their teachings.

THE APOSTLES' CREED

I believe in God, the Father Almighty,
the Creator of heaven and earth,
and in Jesus Christ, his only Son, our Lord;
Who was conceived by the Holy Spirit,
born of the Virgin Mary,
suffered under Pontius Pilate,
was crucified, dead, and buried.
[He descended into hell.] *(Some versions of the Apostles' Creed
don't include this phrase.)*
The third day he arose again from the dead.
He ascended into heaven
and sits at the right hand of God the Father Almighty,
whence he shall come to judge the living and the dead.
I believe in the Holy Spirit,
the holy universal Church,
the communion of saints,
the forgiveness of sins,
the resurrection of the body,
and the life everlasting.
Amen.

MORE TO
EXPLORE

If you'd like to learn more summaries of what the Bible teaches, you may want to read *Big Truths for Young Hearts* by Bruce Ware and *The Ology* by Marty Machowski.

Take time to re-read these summaries. Prayerfully think about what you're reading. Ask God to help you understand the truth in your mind and love it in your heart.

WHAT DO YOU BELIEVE?

Before tablets and computers, most kids learned stuff by reading books. But for nearly all of human history, students learned—about science, math, history, and even the Bible—by hearing and reciting their lessons *out loud*.

When applied to God's Word, this practice became known as "catechizing," which comes from a Greek word meaning, "to teach by speaking." You can find this word (translated "instructed" or "taught") in the Bible (Acts 18:25; 1 Corinthians 14:19; and Galatians 6:6).

In 1529, Martin Luther (see page 149 for more on him) made this method of learning Scripture quite popular, when he published his *Small Catechism*. Using a question-and-answer format, Luther's *Catechism* created a tidal wave of interest in the Bible and also in catechisms.

In the 500 years since Luther, dozens of catechisms have been written: *A Catechism for Young Children* (1652), *The Philadelphia Baptist Catechism* (1742), and *A Catechism of Bible Teaching* (1892). Yet two of the oldest catechisms are still the most famous: *The Heidelberg Catechism* (1563) and *The Westminster Shorter Catechism* (1648).

Everyone ought to memorize at least the first question of both *The Heidelberg Catechism* and *The Westminster Shorter Catechism*. If you absorb these truths into your life, you'll never be the same.

HEIDELBERG CATECHISM

Question #1: What is your only comfort in life and death?

Answer: That I am not my own, but belong–body and soul, in life and in death–to my faithful Savior, Jesus Christ.

WESTMINSTER SHORTER CATECHISM

Question #1: What is the chief end of man?

Answer: Man's chief end is to glorify God and to enjoy him forever.

48

HOW TO MAKE POTTERY

But now, O Lord, you are our Father; we are the clay, and you are our potter; we are all the work of your hand.
Isaiah 64:8

I'll admit it. I like to drink my coffee in a mug made out of dirt. And I'm not alone.

For thousands of years, human beings have crafted all sorts of helpful objects—bowls, jars, cups, plates, lamps, jugs, bricks, and writing tablets—out of clay (which is basically dirt).

Here's the process that a potter (a maker of clay pots) would've used in ancient times: He or she would dig some clay out of a riverbank, knead it into a soft lump, then mold it into whatever he wanted to create. After the potter was finished shaping the clay, he or she would bake it in the sun or in an oven, which would change the object from something soft and bendable into something hard and useful.

Did you know the Bible compares God to a potter? Like a potter, God created humans from the dirt of the ground (Genesis 2:7). And since he is our Creator, he has the right to mold us into whatever he wants us to be (Jeremiah 18:1–6).

As "Potter" and Maker, God loves each of his children. He has made you exactly the way he wanted, with a special plan for you in mind. You can trust this Potter. He has the right to do whatever he wants with your life, but it is always for your good (Romans 8:28).

Use this recipe to try a little pottery too.

Salt Dough

INGREDIENTS:

2 cups flour

1 cup salt

2 tablespoons vegetable oil

3/4 –1 cup hot water

Optional:
food coloring; acrylic paints; toothpicks or other objects for decorating your creation

INSTRUCTIONS:

1. Mix together in a bowl the flour and salt.

2. Add the oil, and then slowly stir in enough water to make a soft, non-sticky dough. If you want to color the dough, add food coloring. Divide up the dough if you want to use several colors.

3. Knead the dough and form it into whatever shape you wish. If you wish to make beads for stringing or something to hang on the wall, make a hole with a toothpick before baking. Important: Keep your project on the thin side—1/2 inch or less—so that it will bake without cracking.

4. Preheat the oven to 250 F degrees.

5. Arrange your creations on a foil-covered cookie sheet. Bake for 1 hour or until hard and dry. Times can vary depending on the thickness of the item.

6. Let cool completely. If you wish, decorate with acrylic paint.

MONEY IN THE BIBLE

Do your parents give you an allowance or spending money? How much do you get? If you lived in Bible times, do you know how much you might get? Would it be one mite a week? A quadran? How about a couple mina? The names and values of these coins sound strange to us today. So, let's figure out how much they were worth.

Matthew tells us that an average worker would earn one denarius (or drachma) per day (Matthew 20:2). Today in the US, a worker might earn $64.00 for a day's work. That's about $8.00 per hour for 8 hours of work. So, let's say that in today's money, a denarius would be worth about $64.00.

Another coin, a mina (also called a pound) was worth 100 denarii (the plural of denarius). And wealth was also measured by a 75-pound unit known as a talent, which was worth about *6,000* denarii!

Then there were also coins having a value less than a denarius. You would have to collect about 64 quadran (or farthings) to equal only one denarius. And your pockets would be bulging if you carried the 128 mites (or leptons) it took to equal a single denarius.

So, here's about how much all these would be worth in today's world.

| 1 mite (lepton) | $0.50 | Mark 12:42 (translated "copper coin") |
| 1 quadran (farthing) | $1.00 | Mark 12:42 (translated "penny") |

How much gold, silver, and bronze did people give to make the tabernacle in the desert?

Answer: Over 1 ton of gold, 3.75 tons of silver, and 2.5 tons of bronze (Exodus 38:24–29)

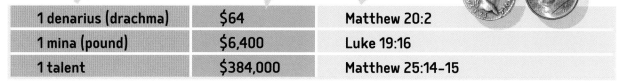

1 denarius (drachma)	$64	Matthew 20:2
1 mina (pound)	$6,400	Luke 19:16
1 talent	$384,000	Matthew 25:14–15

Now stop and rethink these Bible stories, using the modern money values given above.

In Matthew 25:14–30, the "one talent" servant was given $384,000; the "two talent" servant, $768,000; and the "five talent" servant, $1,920,000!

In Matthew 26:15, Judas Iscariot betrays Jesus to get 30 "pieces of silver." The Bible doesn't say exactly which coin was used, but some people think it was a 4-drachma coin (called a tetradrachm), which was worth 4 days' wages. Thirty of these coins would equal about 120 days' or four months' wages. At a modern-day rate of $64 per day, Jesus was betrayed for about $7,680.

In Luke 10:35, the Good Samaritan gave over $120 to pay for the expenses of the man who had been beaten up.

In Matthew 18:23–35, the unforgiving servant had been forgiven a massive debt: 10,000 talents. (That's equal to $3,840,000,000—nearly **4 billion dollars** or over 164,000 years of work!) But this servant was not willing to forgive the man who only owed him 100 denarii ($6,400 or 100 days of work).

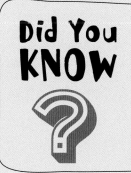

Did You KNOW ?

A US dollar bill is 0.0043 inches thick. If you made a stack of 64 dollar bills (which equals 1 denarius), your pile of cash would stand just over ¼ inch tall. One mina of dollar bills would be over 2 feet tall (27.5 inches). And a stack of dollar bills equaling one talent would be taller than a 12-story building (1,651 inches)!

50

HOW TO MAKE GOOD DECISIONS

"What should I do?" said Makayla, as she looked at the two invitations in her hands. "Should I go to the birthday party at a friend's house or the game night at church?"

The choice wasn't easy. Makayla had been trying to be a good friend to a girl at school who wasn't a Christian. And now this girl had invited Makayla to her birthday party. At the same time, Makayla's best friends were at church, and she had been looking forward to this church activity for a long time.

What should she do? What did God want her to do? Did God even have an opinion? How would she decide? Decisions aren't always simple, and as you get older, you will have even more decisions to make:

"I got $65 for my birthday. How should I spend it?"

"Which sport should I play?"

"My friend has been doing 'stupid stuff,' what should I do?"

"I'm not allowed to use the Internet when my parents aren't home. Is it OK to go online just to get my homework?"

"I wonder what God wants me to be when I grow up."

Here are some Bible truths to remember when you have to make a decision:

1. Make your choice based on what God says. If God says in the Bible not to do something (like steal, cheat, lie, be mean, etc.), then you know for sure not to do it. Of course you still need his help to listen and obey, but now at least you know what's wrong and what's right. (Verse to read: James 4:17)

2. Choose to please God. The more you know God, the better you will know what he likes. For example, God loves mercy. So, if you have two options to pick from, and one is more merciful, then this merciful option would usually be a better choice. (Verses to read: Ephesians 5:8-10)

3. Ask for help. Of course you can't do the first two things without God right there with you, helping you. Ask him for wisdom and he will give it! Then ask others for help too—parents, a pastor, a youth group leader, and friends you trust. (Verses to read: James 1:5-6)

4. After all this, make your decision knowing that God will guide you *through* your decision-making. (Verses to read: Proverbs 16:1, 9, 20)

5. You will not make perfect decisions, but God is always in control. You may (or may not!) be confident about your decisions. But you can always trust the Lord: he has promised to guide you. (Verses to read: Matthew 10:29-30)

THINK ABOUT IT

Are you asking God for wisdom?

Are you thinking about the options?

Are you asking for help from others?

Are you trusting God to guide you?

Are you obeying what God has commanded?

Are you seeking to please God?

Then, what decision will you make?

51

FUN AND GAMES IN BIBLE TIMES

C hildren in ancient times, just like today, loved playing games and having fun. They played board games with names like: "Mehen," "Senet," and "Dogs and Jackals." Did you know that even the Bible talks about fun and games? Here is some of the fun stuff the Bible mentions:

Wrestling opponents (Genesis 32:24–26)
Shooting arrows (1 Samuel 20:20)
Telling riddles (Judges 14:18)
Playing outside (Zechariah 8:5)
Dancing joyfully (Job 21:11–12)
Recounting stories (Psalm 78:3–4)
Running races (1 Corinthians 9:24)
Making puns (Judges 15:16)
Taking walks (Psalm 23:2–3)
Racing chariots (Philippians 3:13–14)
Playing pretend (Matthew 11:17)
Playing music (Luke 7:32)
Boxing opponents (1 Corinthians 9:26)
Camping out (Nehemiah 8:17–18)

Throwing parties (Esther 9:19)
Giving nicknames (Mark 3:17)
Enjoying animals (Job 41:5)

The Bible teaches that there is a time for everything. There's a right time for fun and games and play and laughing (Ecclesiastes 3:4). Growing up is a time to get ready for being an adult, but it's time for some fun too (1 Corinthians 13:11). Here's a game you can enjoy with a friend or family member!

Dogs and Jackals

No one knows for certain how "Dogs and Jackals" was played in ancient times. But here is one way it might have been played.

What You Need: Color copy of game board; piece of Styrofoam or foam core board the same size as the game board; glue or tape; ten toothpicks for game pieces; three pennies.

Assemble the game board by using glue or tape to attach the copy of the game board to the piece of Styrofoam. Now you're ready to play.

Object: Players sit on opposite sides of the game board. One side is for Dogs, the other for Jackals. Each player has their own set of holes numbered 1 through 29. Each player takes five toothpicks and inserts them into holes 1 through 5. The object of the game is to move all five toothpicks around the board and exit at hole 29. The first player to get all toothpicks off the board, wins.

Photo-copy game board from the next page!

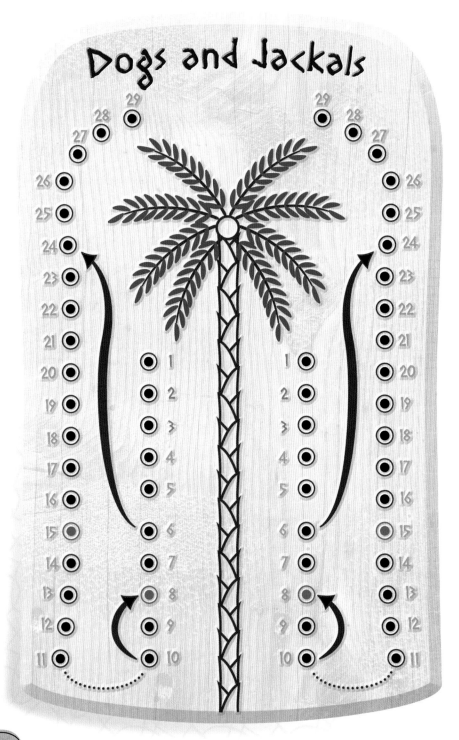

RULES OF PLAY:

1. On your turn, toss three pennies and move as follows:

▶ If you toss **one head**, move one toothpick, one hole.

▶ If you toss **two heads**, move one toothpick, two holes.

▶ If you toss **three heads**, move one toothpick, three holes.

▶ If you toss **three tails**, move one toothpick, five holes.

2. You may only move one toothpick during a turn. You may not move a second toothpick until the first one passes hole 11. You may not move your third toothpick until the second toothpick passes hole 11, etc. *(Alternate Rule: Or you can just race one toothpick at a time, from start to finish. In other words, your second toothpick cannot move until your first one exits at hole 29.)*

3. Two toothpicks may not occupy the same hole. If a player cannot make a move, play passes to the other player.

4. If your toothpick lands in a hole connected to a curvy line (or "slide"), ride the slide **in the direction of the arrow** to the hole at the other end of the curvy line. *(Alternate Rule: You can also change the direction of the arrows to create other ways to play.)*

5. If you land in a blue hole, you get a free turn. *(Alternate Rule: Or if you land in a blue hole, you lose a turn.)*

LEARN THE GREEK ALPHABET

The Greek language was the most common written language in the Roman Empire when Jesus was born.

It's all Greek to me!

Many people in Jesus's day—from soldiers to servants, and young to old—knew Greek. Even if people spoke other languages, they still knew and understood Greek. In fact, the entire Old Testament, which had been written in Hebrew, was then also translated into Greek. God had caused this one language to spread so that the good news about Jesus could be understood throughout the Roman Empire.

So, when the New Testament was written in the first century, it too was written in Greek. And its authors wrote using everyday words. All this allowed most of the humans alive at that time to be able to understand God's Word when it was read.

You can learn a little Greek, too. Using the chart (on the next page), start by trying to memorize three things: (1) the lowercase Greek letters, (2) the names of the letters, and (3) which English letters they match. (Here are some hints and helps: some letters sound kind of similar, which makes them easy to

UPPER CASE	LOWER CASE	NAME	SOUND	ENGLISH EQUIVALENT
A	α	alpha (AL-fuh)	a as in Aslan	a
B	β	beta (BAY-tuh)	b as in Bilbo	b
Γ	γ	gamma (GA-muh)	g as in Gandalf	g
Δ	δ	delta (DEL-tuh)	d as in Dori	d
E	ε	epsilon (EP-sill-onn)	e as in Edmund	short e
Z	ζ	zeta (ZAY-tuh)	z as in Miraz	z
H	η	eta (AY-tuh)	e as in Theoden	long e or a
Θ	θ	theta (THAY-tuh)	th as in Thorin	th
I	ι	iota (YOH-tuh; not yoda)	i as in Isildur	short i
K	κ	kappa (KA-puh)	k as in Ketterley	k
Λ	λ	lambda (LAM-duh)	l as in Legolas	l
M	μ	mu (MOO)	m as in Macready	m
N	ν	nu (NOO)	n as in Nori	n
Ξ	ξ	xi (KZEE)	x as in Shadowfax	x
O	o	omicron (AHM-uh-kronn)	o as in Octesian	short o
Π	π	pi (PEE)	p as in Pevensie	p
P	ρ	rho (ROW)	r as in Reepicheep	r
Σ	σ or ς	sigma (SIGG-muh)	s as in Sam	s
T	τ	tau (TOW, as in cow)	t as in Tumnus	t
Υ	υ	upsilon (OOP-sill-onn)	yu as in Eustace	long u
Φ	φ	phi (FEE)	f as in Frodo	f
X	χ	chi (KEE)	k as in Kili	ch
Ψ	ψ	psi (PSEE)	ps as in maps	ps
Ω	ω	omega (oh-MAY-guh)	o as in Oakenshield	long o

memorize together. For example, ze*ta*, e*ta*, the*ta*, io*ta*; or *phi*, *chi*, *psi*. It also helps that many of the letters follow the order of the English alphabet: *lambda*, *mu*, *nu*; or *omicron*, *pi*, *rho*, *sigma*, *tau*, *upsilon*.)

Once you've memorized the alphabet, test yourself. See if you can write all the lower case letters in order in less than 60 seconds. Go!

Decipher which English words are written below with Greek letters.

Βιβλε_____

σταρ_____

κωβρα_____

Θινκ_____

ψαλμ_____

δραγον_____

Try to figure out this message. It's in English, but written with Greek letters.

Ιν θε φωρτ

Νηδ μωρε πηοπλε

Βρινγ γαμε ανδ πεππερονι πιζζα ανδ εξτρα βρεαδ στιξ

Βη φαστ!

Now it's your turn. Can you write your own secret message to a friend using only Greek letters?

Did You KNOW

By the time Jesus was born, God had perfectly prepared the world for the spread of the gospel. From 25 B.C to A.D. 180, the civilized world enjoyed the prosperity and peace of the Pax Romana ("Roman peace"). No major wars would keep the news of Jesus Christ from spreading rapidly throughout the civilized world.

Long before this, in 500 B.C., Rome began constructing its famous system of roads, which eventually spanned some 250,000 miles connecting 113 provinces. Within this empire there were no national borders to cross or passports to carry. As a result, 2.5 million square miles and many different nations and cultures were open and accessible to early gospel missionaries.

53

EATING WITH JESUS

Family get-togethers are great (except for all the comments about how tall you're getting and your aunt's perfume). Of course, you're always part of your family, but these reunions are special celebrations filled with fun, laughter, stories, and food!

Did you know that the church has a celebration like this too? It's called Communion or the Lord's Supper. As a Christian, you're part of God's family 24/7, but Communion is a special time together as a church. Often it is held once a month and in some churches every Sunday. The Lord's Supper can seem confusing—there's a drink and some kind of bread. People pray and sing together. What's it all about? Here are some of the basics:

Since you're part of his family, God promises you wonderful things, which is part of an agreement called a "covenant." The Lord promises that you are now part of his people and that he will be your God. He will be with you and take care of you, like a loving father cares for his children.

In the Bible, these "covenants" are often celebrated with a meal (Genesis 31:43–54). In

Who held the longest celebration in the Bible?
King Ahasuerus held a celebration that lasted for 180 days (Esther 1:3–4).

Exodus God made a covenant (called "the old covenant") with his people. Moses said,

"Look, this blood confirms the covenant the Lord has made with you in giving you these instructions. Then Moses . . . and the seventy elders of Israel climbed up the mountain. There they saw the God of Israel. . . . And though these nobles of Israel gazed upon God, he did not destroy them. In fact, they ate a covenant meal, eating and drinking in his presence!" (Exodus 24:8–11 NLT)

And this is also what happened in the New Testament when *Jesus* made a covenant with his people, the "*new* covenant." And like the Old Testament covenant, this new covenant also included a meal. At this feast ("the Last Supper"), which Jesus ate with his disciples, he took the cup and said, "This is my blood of the covenant, which is poured out for many for the forgiveness of sins" (Matthew 26:28; also read Luke 22:20).

All Christians today are part of God's new covenant people—those who trust Jesus's death for the forgiveness of sin. And this means that we also have a seat at his table as his dearly loved children. So when your church celebrates the Lord's Supper, you're actually enjoying a new covenant meal. Just like you enjoy meals and stories with your own family, Communion is a special time for God's people to remember and give thanks for Jesus and how he shed his blood to forgive their sins. At the Lord's Supper we celebrate with Jesus, who has promised to join us at the table (Matthew 18:20).

WE EAT.

WE REMEMBER.

WE ENJOY.

54

THE BEST WAY TO DEAL WITH YOUR ENEMIES

If you've read much of the Old Testament, you know that God's people always had enemies. Israel faced the Egyptians, the Philistines, the Midianites, the Assyrians, the Persians, and the list could go on.

In almost every situation, the same basic story happened again and again. An enemy would attack God's people, and sometimes the enemy would win. Then life would be pretty miserable.

So God's people would pray! They'd beg him to rescue them. And in different ways, God would send deliverers to rescue his people. These were people like Moses, David, Gideon, and Esther.

In some of these cases, God's people just waited, praying for God to deliver them (think Moses and the escape from Egypt). Other times, God's people took action by serving wisely even inside the enemy's government (think Esther and the Persians, or Daniel in Babylon). Then there were times when God's people fought their enemies, actually picking up swords, slings, or spears (think Joshua or David).

When Jesus came along, God's people still had an enemy: the Roman Empire.

The Romans were crushing God's people with slavery, poverty, taxes, and temptations to sin. And as always, many of God's people were praying that the Lord would rescue them and defeat their enemy. But how would God go about doing it? No one knew exactly. As in the Old Testament, there were three basic approaches that were popular in Jesus's day—each way was followed by a different group of people mentioned in the New Testament.

GROUP 1: DON'T ROCK THE BOAT

The "Sadducees" were rich and powerful leaders of Israel who hung out with the governing Roman authorities and, like Esther or Daniel, hoped to use their position of power to influence the enemy. Because the Sadducees didn't actually believe many things in the Bible, they ended up just wanting to hang onto their leadership positions. So the Sadducees didn't change Rome. Rome changed them. They didn't turn out to be like Esther or Daniel at all.

GROUP 2: BE AS HOLY AS YOU CAN

Today, the word Pharisee is used to describe a proud hypocrite, but in New Testament times, the Pharisees, like Ezra and Nehemiah in the Old Testament, wanted everyone to keep God's law. If God's people were good enough, the Pharisees believed that God would hear their prayers and come defeat Rome. Sadly, however, the Pharisees tried to obey God's Word with their actions, but their hearts were far from God himself. They weren't really like Ezra and Nehemiah at all.

GROUP 3: PICK UP YOUR SWORD

The "Zealots" were the Robin Hoods of Jesus's day! Like the famous heroes of the Old Testament, they wanted Israel to rise up and fight the enemy (Rome). If all God's people would join the fight, then God would come down and defeat the enemy just as in ancient times. Yet Rome defeated Israel every time they tried to fight. The approach of the Zealots was a far cry from famous victories won by Joshua, Samson, and David.

GOD'S RADICAL APPROACH

But God had a new approach, a revolutionary one. And it took almost everyone by surprise. The Lord would handle his enemies—not by influencing, fighting, or staying separate from them—but *by serving them and dying for them*! Jesus, the Rescuer, healed people—including Romans! (Matthew 8:5–13) He even forgave the sin of the enemy (Luke 23:24). How did he do this?

Jesus defeated the enemy by giving his life to turn them into friends (Romans 12:20). Carefully read Romans 5:6–11, noting all the changes brought by Jesus's death. As you read, remember that *we ourselves* used to be enemies of God

(Romans 5:9). But instead of crushing us, Jesus let himself be crushed in our place—taking our punishment (Romans 5:10) and making God our deepest delight (Romans 5:11).

And since he's made us friends, we now get to share his love with others—even with the "enemies" in your life. Listen to these words of Jesus: "Love your enemies and pray for those who persecute you" (Matthew 5:44). This is how Jesus treated his enemies, and he wants us to live the same way.

WHEN we were utterly helpless, Christ came at just the right time and died for us sinners. Now, most people would not be willing to die for an upright person, though someone might perhaps be willing to die for a person who is especially good. But God showed his great love for us by sending Christ to die for us while we were still sinners. And since we have been made right in God's sight by the blood of Christ, he will certainly save us from God's condemnation. For since our friendship with God was restored by the death of his Son while we were still his enemies, we will certainly be saved through the life of his Son. So now we can rejoice in our wonderful new relationship with God because our Lord Jesus Christ has made us friends of God. (Romans 5:6–11 NLT)

Are there people who dislike you, annoy you, or just drive you crazy? Ask the Lord to help you think of at least five new ways you can love and serve them. What'll happen when you do this? You never know: you may find that your enemies have turned into friends.

55

DID JESUS *REALLY* RISE FROM THE DEAD?

esus's resurrection is like a fork in the road. When you come to a fork in the road, to keep going forward you have to choose either one path or another. When we come to the resurrection, we also have to choose—but this choice is about what we believe. People will either believe that Jesus is God and that he actually physically rose from the dead, defeating death for all who believe, or they will turn away and reject the Bible and Jesus as false (1 Corinthians 15:14, 17).

Here are some facts the Bible gives that demonstrate that Jesus really did rise from the dead, just as he promised he would.

1 The Empty Tomb

Everyone, even the people who killed Jesus, agreed that the tomb was empty (Matthew 28:11–15). If the tomb had *not* been empty, then the enemies of Jesus could have proved he hadn't risen by simply pointing to Jesus's body still lying in his tomb. So, this only leaves two options: Jesus's body was either (1) raised by God or (2) stolen by people.

2 The Lying Guards

The Roman soldiers who guarded Jesus's tomb said that while they were asleep, Jesus's disciples stole the body (Matthew 28:13). But if the guards were sleeping, how could they have possibly seen or known what had happened? Obviously, the soldier's story—about Jesus's body being stolen—is a lie.

3 The Eyewitnesses

All four Gospels provide eyewitness accounts of several women who went to Jesus's tomb early in the morning of his resurrection (Matthew 28:1–8; Mark 16:1–8; Luke 24:1–11; John 20:1–2). In the Roman world, women were not allowed to give eyewitness testimony in court. So, if the disciples were making up a story about Jesus's resurrection, why would they have used women as eyewitnesses—unless it's what actually happened!

4 The Dying Disciples

What kind of person would be willing to be killed for something they *knew* was just a lie? No one (1 Corinthians 15:14, 19). If the disciples had agreed to lie about Jesus's resurrection, then surely when thrown into prison one of them would have said, "Don't kill me. We just made it up. The resurrection never took place." But that didn't happen (Acts 5:26–33). Their report of the resurrection must be genuine.

5 The Verifiable Records

Almost everyone agrees that the four Gospels were all written within 30–60 years of Jesus's death. That means that if Matthew, Mark, Luke, and John were trying to trick everyone by spreading lies about the resurrection, then many people who first read these books would have remembered what had really happened. And these people would have spread the word that the stories about the resurrection were all a bunch of lies. But that didn't happen. The story wasn't disproved. In fact, the resurrection was true, and hundreds of people had been there, had seen the resurrected Jesus, and knew that the facts written in the Gospels had actually happened.

56

GRASPING THE GOSPELS

What's your best friend like? Could you draw a picture of him or her? Depending on someone's age and skill, she might quickly sketch a one-dimensional stick figure or sit down to paint a more-detailed portrait. A great artist can even bring a painting to life by making a two-dimensional drawing look three-dimensional, adding depth to length and breadth.

When God wanted to paint a portrait of his Son, he didn't do it in 2D or even 3D, but 4D! There are four books we call the Gospels: Matthew, Mark, Luke, and John. Each one tells the story of the life, death, and resurrection of Jesus Christ. But like four cameras focused on the same object from four different angles, each Gospel writer tells the same story but from his own perspective.

Did You KNOW

Over the centuries, Christians have also identified each Gospel with a special symbol. Matthew is represented by a man with wings, which points to the fact that the Son of God became a human being. Mark is symbolized by a lion with wings, showing that Jesus is the mighty King. Luke is identified by an ox with wings, showing that Jesus is the strong, yet humble sacrifice for sin. And John is signified by an eagle, representing Jesus as the exalted Son from heaven.

MATTHEW

emphasis about Jesus

Length

How Long: Much like a news reporter, *Matthew* looks back over the length of Old Testament history and shows that Jesus is the long-awaited Messiah (Matthew 5:17). When you read, look for how Jesus came to fulfill all that the Old Testament had promised.

Writing Style

Reporter

28
Chapters

Key Verses
1:21, 28:18-20
She will give birth to a son, and you are to give him the name Jesus, because he will save his people from their sins.
Matthew 1:21

MARK

emphasis about Jesus

Depth

How Deep: *Mark* tells the action-packed story of how Jesus humbled himself to come down and "give his life a ransom for many" (Mark 10:45). When you read, pay attention to how often Jesus talks about his death.

Writing Style

Storyteller

16
Chapters

Key Verse
10:45
For even the Son of Man did not come to be served, but to serve, and to give his life as a ransom for many.

LUKE

emphasis about Jesus

Breadth

How Broad: Like the scientist he is (he is a doctor), *Luke* precisely records the breadth of the Savior's love (Luke 19:9-10). When you read, notice that Jesus came to save a wide variety of people: the poor, sick, weak, little—all who are lost.

Writing Style

Historian

24
Chapters

Key Verses
2:11; 19:10
For the Son of Man came to seek and to save the lost.
Luke 19:10

JOHN

emphasis about Jesus

Height

How High: *John*, using simple words that point to big truth, tells how Jesus, the exalted Son of God, came from the heights of heaven to show the world God the Father and open the way to him (John 14:6). When you read, be on the lookout for how Jesus shows the glory of the most high God.

Writing Style

Theologian

21
Chapters

Key Verses
1:14; 3:16; 20:30-31
For God so loved the world that he gave his one and only Son, that whoever believes in him shall not perish but have eternal life.
John 3:16

THE ACTS OF JESUS— CONTINUED

Luke also wrote a sequel to his Gospel: the Book of Acts. The first half of Acts (1:1—12:24) shows how the Good News about Jesus went out to all kinds of people: to Jews, semi-Jews (like the Samaritans), and non-Jews (the Gentiles).

The second half of Acts (12:25—28:31) shows how the gospel exploded geographically. from one country to the next, from Jerusalem all the way to Rome (1,434 miles away)!

57

KNOTS YOU CAN'T UNTIE

Alexander the Great was a young man with a problem. He wanted to conquer all of Asia Minor (modern-day Turkey), but his army hadn't yet won any great battles. So, he needed a victory to rally his troops. He needed something to prove that he was strong enough to rule all of Asia Minor.

Then he came to the city of Gordium. According to legend, old King Gordius had tied a strange knot so complicated no one could untie it. In fact, it was said that whoever could untie this knot would become ruler of all Asia Minor.

So it was that in 33 B.C. Alexander began to work on untying this legendary knot. But the knot couldn't be untied. Finally, he grabbed his sword and cut the knot in half. In time, all of Asia Minor fell under Alexander the Great's control.

You may never be faced with having to untie a Gordian knot. In fact, if you work at it, you can untie almost any knot. (Try tying and untying these knots.)

But did you know the Bible talks about some knots you can *never* untie? God's Word teaches that every human being is tied to either Adam or Jesus. There is no other option.

Every person is born with a humanly unbreakable link to the first human being, Adam. He sinned in the Garden of Eden, and we are all connected to him. So what was true of Adam is also true of us, his descendants. When he

KNOTS

How to Tie a Square Knot
(An easy knot for tying two ropes together)

A Bowline Knot
(A knot to create a loop at the end of a rope)

A Half-Hitch Knot
(A knot for tying a rope to an object)

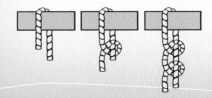

sinned, we sinned (Romans 5:12). That means that all of us, even you, are born sinful and guilty. Why? Not because you did sinful things (though we all do). Instead, you're a sinner because you are roped up with Adam's first sin.

But every person who is born *again* (John 3:3) has been loosed by God from Adam and his sin and has been bound to Jesus (called the "last Adam" in 1 Corinthians 15:45). Unlike the first Adam, Jesus always obeyed God the Father. And since all Christians are connected to Jesus, then, amazingly, what is true of him is also true of all Christians.

WHEN HE OBEYED, WE OBEYED.
(ROMANS 5:19)

WHEN HE DIED TO SIN, WE DIED TO SIN.
(ROMANS 6:3–4)

AND WHEN HE WAS RAISED TO NEW LIFE, SO WERE WE.
(ROMANS 6:8–9)

So if you're a Christian, God considers you righteous and beloved. You can come to the Father whenever you want. You will enjoy life with him forever (Romans 5:1–2). Why? Not because you are good or worthy. But because you are "in Christ"—connected to him—tied to him and his righteousness.

Some people who study the Bible call this connection to Jesus: "union with Christ." And because you're united to Jesus, the Father always treats you like he treats his Son. And this union will never be untied.

58

EIGHT DAYS THAT CHANGED THE WORLD

What if you wanted to learn more about Abraham Lincoln? What would you do? If you were in a hurry, you could do a quick search on the Internet. But if you wanted to learn more, you could go to a library, check out a biography about the 16th US President, find a comfy chair, and start to read.

You'd read a chapter about his family and how Abe grew up. Another chapter or two would cover his early career as a lawyer and then as a senator from the state of Illinois. Finally, you'd read how he became president and led the nation through the Civil War. Then several chapters would tell the sad story of his assassination. When you finished the book, you'd know a lot about every period of this famous man's life.

But this is *not* how Jesus's biographies were written. The Gospel writers (Matthew, Mark, Luke, and John) tell a little about Jesus's birth and almost nothing about his childhood. Instead, the action really gets going when Jesus is baptized at about 30 years of age. After that, Jesus preaches and performs miracles for about three years. But the four Gospels mostly focus on just *one week* of Jesus's life: from the Sunday Jesus entered Jerusalem until the next Sunday when he rose from the dead. These were eight days that changed human history.

How much of their books do the Gospel writers devote to that last week of Jesus's ministry? Matthew, 8 chapters; Mark, 6 chapters; Luke, 6 chapters; and

John, 9 chapters. That means that 29 chapters (about one-third of all the chapters in the Gospels) talk about the last days of Jesus's earthly life and ministry. This last week is known as "Passion Week"; the Latin word, *passio*, means "suffering." (See pages 96–97 to learn more Latin words and phrases.)

So why do the Gospel writers spend so much time on this single week? A clue lies in the fact that Jesus didn't come to earth only as a teacher and a healer. He came to die. All his journeys were ultimately heading toward the cross. Jesus said, "The Son of Man came not to be served but to serve, and to give his life as a ransom for many" (Mark 10:45). And human history has never been the same.

EIGHT DAYS THAT CHANGED THE WORLD

1 DAY 1
SUNDAY

Palm Sunday

Riding into Jerusalem on a donkey as the prophet said he would (Zechariah 9:9), Jesus is welcomed by joyful crowds shouting, "Hosanna to the Son of David! Blessed is he who comes in the name of the Lord!" (Mt. 21:9)

Verses to Read:
Mt. 21:1–11; Mk. 11:1–11; Lk. 19:28–44; Jn. 12:12–19

2 DAY 2
MONDAY

Clearing the temple

Finding the temple court full of buyers and sellers, Jesus throws them out and overturns their tables.

Verses to Read:
Mt. 21:10–17; Mk. 11:15–18; Lk. 19:45–48

3 DAY 3
TUESDAY

Day of teaching

Jesus, telling parables, warns the people about the Pharisees. He tells of things that will happen in the future.

Verses to Read:
Mt. 21:23–24:51; Mk. 11:27–13:37; Lk. 20:1–21:36

DAY 4
WEDNESDAY

Day of Rest

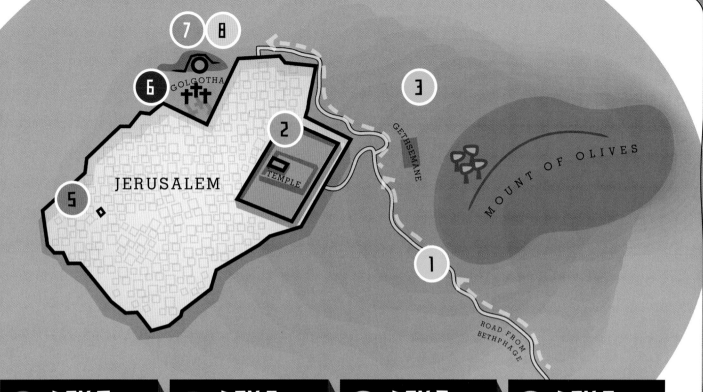

5 DAY 5
THURSDAY

Last Supper

In the upper room, gathered with his disciples to eat the Passover meal, Jesus begins the tradition that we call the Lord's Supper. The bread is his body that will be sacrificed, and the drink represents his blood that will be shed. Afterwards, they go to the Garden of Gethsemane to watch and pray.

Verses to Read:
Mt. 26:17–30;
Mk. 14:12–26;
Lk. 22:7–23; Jn. 13:1–30

6 DAY 6
FRIDAY

Crucifixion

Jesus is betrayed, arrested, tried, condemned to death, beaten, and finally, carrying his cross, is led to Golgotha ("the place of the skull") to be crucified.

Verses to Read:
Mt. 27:1–61;
Mk. 15:1–47;
Lk. 22:66–23:56;
Jn. 18:28–19:37

7 DAY 7
SATURDAY

The Sabbath

Jesus's body lies in the tomb.

Verses to Read:
Mt. 27:62–66,
Lk. 23:56

8 DAY 8
SUNDAY

Resurrection

Just as he said, Jesus was raised from the dead.

Verses to Read:
Mt. 20:1–13;
Mk. 16:1–20;
Lk. 24:1–49;
Jn. 20:1–31

219

59

ANCIENT TEXTING

How long does it take to send a text to a friend who lives hundreds of miles away? It takes no time at all. It is immediate. Your friend will get your text as long as she has her phone handy. (In fact, a text message can cross the Pacific Ocean in 1/20ᵗʰ of a second!)

But in ancient Rome, the fastest way to communicate was through writing letters. Thanks to the Roman road system and postal service, a letter could travel from 50 to 150 miles per day (depending on how urgent it was). For example, a letter from Rome could travel the 1,676 miles to the northern part of the Empire (modern-day London) in about 22 days (roughly 77 miles per day).

The followers of Jesus also used letters to spread the Good News of God's Word. We still have copies of these letters (also called "epistles"). Out of the 27 books in the New Testament, 21 of them are letters—basically all the books from Romans to Jude. (Revelation is also a letter, in addition to being a special kind of book called "apocalyptic literature," see page 9.) Most of these letters follow the same basic, letter-writing format used in that time period.

But why were Jesus's apostles sending these letters? They wanted to help Christians (and their churches) all across the Roman Empire. If

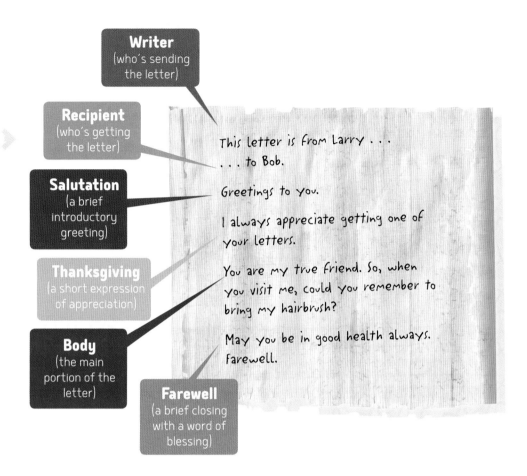

Writer (who's sending the letter)

Recipient (who's getting the letter)

Salutation (a brief introductory greeting)

Thanksgiving (a short expression of appreciation)

Body (the main portion of the letter)

Farewell (a brief closing with a word of blessing)

This letter is from Larry . . .

. . . to Bob.

Greetings to you.

I always appreciate getting one of your letters.

You are my true friend. So, when you visit me, could you remember to bring my hairbrush?

May you be in good health always. Farewell.

you read the letters, you'll see that these believers struggled with three basic problems:

1 **Bad living.** Christians struggled to live like God's people in the face of temptation.

2 **Bad teaching.** Christians struggled to live like God's people in the face of error.

3 **Bad treatment.** Christians struggled to live like God's people in the face of persecution.

Letters in the Roman Empire were usually written on long sheets of papyrus, a paper made from the papyrus plant. To pen their letters, writers took an 8- to 10-inch-long reed with a sharp tip and dipped it into red or black ink before applying it to the papyrus. Since the black ink was

not waterproof, and could smudge or smear easily, important letters were often written in the more expensive red ink and/or carried inside leather containers.

The apostles wrote letters to explain how the Good News about Jesus can help in all the struggles these believers would face. They show how Jesus's life, death, and resurrection bring new meaning to their everyday lives. The letters do this in two ways: they remind Christians of what is *true*—of what Jesus has already done for them. The letters also tell Christians what *to do*—how to live out the gospel.

Every New Testament letter contains both the **true** and the **to do** parts. But in the Letters of Romans, Ephesians, and Colossians, these sections are super easy to find.

What is true	What to do
Romans 1–11	Romans 12–16
Ephesians 1–3	Ephesians 4–6
Colossians 1–2	Colossians 3–4

When you sit down to read one of the letters in the New Testament, pretend that you just received a leather case in the mail. You open it and find that it contains a rolled-up sheet of papyrus. As you unroll the letter, read its words remembering that they're God's words written directly to you.

WHAT WAS CHURCH LIKE FOR THE FIRST CHRISTIANS?

This underground stone chapel is in Damascus, Syria. It has been in use as a church since before A.D. 500.

Did you ever wonder what church services were like in Bible times?

John, the last living apostle, died around A.D. 95. Less than twenty years later, Pliny (rhymes with *skinny*), a Roman governor in Asia Minor (modern-day Turkey), sent spies into a nearby church. Here is what he discovered and reported in a letter to the Roman emperor Trajan:

> *It was their habit on a fixed day to assemble before daylight and recite by turns a form of words to Christ as a God; and that they bound themselves with an oath . . . not to commit theft or robbery or adultery, [and] not to break their word. After this was done, their custom was to depart and to meet again to take food—but ordinary and harmless food.*

THE EARLY CHURCH

What we would have heard...

What we would have seen...

GOD'S WORD BEING TAUGHT

Acts 2:42;
1 Timothy 4:13

GOD'S WORD BEING READ

1 Timothy 4:13

PRAYING TO THE LORD

Acts 2:42;
1 Timothy 2:8

SINGING IN PRAISE

1 Corinthians 14:26;
Ephesians 5:18–20;
Colossians 3:15–17

REPORTS AND TESTIMONIES BEING GIVEN

Acts 14:27; 15:3–4

money being collected to help others

Acts 2:44–47;
Philippians 4:15

the Lord's Supper being celebrated

Acts 2:42; 20:7;
1 Corinthians
11:16–34

ministry leaders being appointed

Acts 6:1–6; 15:22;
2 Corinthians 8:19

people using spiritual gifts to serve one another

1 Corinthians 14:1,
12, 26

sinners repenting and being restored to fellowship

Matthew 18:15–20;
1 Corinthians 5:1–8

Who knows if Pliny's spies were telling the whole truth. But if we had the chance to observe a New Testament church service for ourselves, we know some things we would have heard and seen. How? The Bible tells us the kinds of things we would have heard and seen on the chart.

But, God said that whatever you did at church—whether you used your gifts, appointed leaders, taught and read the Word, celebrated communion, restored a sinner, prayed to God, gave testimonies or money, or sang—all of these had to be done in *love* (1 Corinthians 13).

When this happens—when love guides all we do in church—we help each other to become more like Jesus. This is why 1 Corinthians 14 reminds us, over and over, to do everything in church so that others are built up and helped (verses 4, 5, 12, 17, 26).

So, the next time you go to church, don't just go to watch. Join in where you can. As a kid, you may not be able to teach the Bible, but you certainly could encourage or show love to someone. Before you go to church this weekend, read 1 Corinthians 13:4 7. Then ask the Lord to help you encourage someone the next time you go to church.

MORE TO EXPLORE ▶ If you'd like to learn more about the history of the church, you may want to read *Christian History Made Easy* by Timothy Paul Jones.

61

HOW DID YOU GET YOUR BIBLE?

The short answer is: God wrote the Bible, and your parents bought it for you. Simple. The long answer is, well, longer. Look at the next page from top to bottom to learn more about how you got your Bible. First, at the top, you'll see that God actively revealed himself to his people. At the bottom of the page, God quietly teaches you what his Word means. In between are the steps that gave you the Bible.

1. REVELATION:
God took action, revealing himself in human history.

Example, God provided a ram for Abraham to sacrifice (Genesis 22; 35:7)

2. INSPIRATION:
God moved people to write about it. The Holy Spirit ensured that what was written was God's own Word.

Example, the Holy Spirit moved Moses to write about Abraham's sacrifice (Deuteronomy 31:9; also see 2 Peter 1:21; 2 Timothy 3:16–17)

3. CANONIZATION:
God guided people to accept the writings he had already inspired.

(Exodus 24:3; also see Joshua 24:26; 1 Corinthians 14:37–38)

4. TRANSMISSION AND PRESERVATION:
People make many duplicate copies of God's Word. God protects his Word, preserving his inspired Word from being lost.

(Deuteronomy 17:18; Joshua 8:32; and Deuteronomy 31:26; 2 Kings 23:24; 2 Peter 3:15–16)

5. TRANSLATION:
God gives people the ability to clearly communicate his Word in many different languages.

(Nehemiah 8:8; Matthew 1:23)

6. ILLUMINATION:
As you read the Bible, God through the Holy Spirit teaches, helps, and changes you through his Word.

(2 Peter 3:16; 2 Timothy 2:7)

62

TAKE NOTE

Did you know that if you go to church once a week, you may hear more than *3,000* sermons before you turn 70 years old? That's a lot of preaching. Why do we listen to sermons at church?

In the Bible, we learn that when God's people hear his Word, their faith grows stronger. Our faith grows as we're reminded of who God is, how much he loves us, what he has done for us, and all he helps us do. (Read Acts 20:31–32.)

Listening to God's Word as it's preached is one way that God grows your faith. So what do you remember about last week's sermon? One way to learn from preaching is to write down what you're hearing. Here are some ideas to help you understand and grow from what you hear.

Get ready. There's no better way to prepare to hear God's Word than to pray. Ask God for the Holy Spirit to teach you; ask him to help you listen well. And don't forget to take a pen or pencil and some paper to write on. You might even want to get a notebook to use each week.

At the beginning of the sermon, start by writing down the basic facts: the speaker's name, the date, and the passage of Scripture. Here are some ways, using the acronym **GOAL**, to benefit from what is being taught in the sermon:

G for God. Keep a list of everything you hear about God. What is God like? What does he love? What has he done? What promises has he made? What has he commanded? and so forth.

O for Outline. Try to follow the speaker's plan or outline. Usually a preacher takes a main theme and develops it with several supporting ideas. So, listen for the main theme and write it down. This is the "big idea"—what it's all about. Then try to follow the flow or outline of the message. Here's an example.

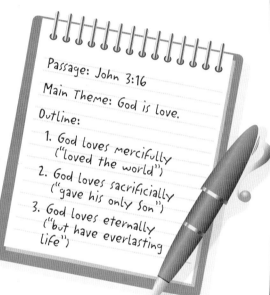

Passage: John 3:16

Main Theme: God is love.

Outline:

1. God loves mercifully ("loved the world")
2. God loves sacrificially ("gave his only Son")
3. God loves eternally ("but have everlasting life")

A for Action. Ask, "How is the Lord leading me to put what I've heard into action?" God wants us to do more than just listen to his Word; he wants us to respond to his Word. Are there promises to trust? commands to obey? truths to believe? sins to confess? Write down your action plan.

L for Later. With the Holy Spirit as your teacher there will be some things you hear that will jump out at you. Jot them down to think about later. And then take time to re-read your notes later in the day or in the week. Each time you think about what you heard, ask God to help you truly believe and obey all he's taught you in his Word.

63

HE [GOD] MADE THE MOON TO MARK THE SEASONS; THE SUN KNOWS ITS TIME FOR SETTING.

PSALM 104:19

HOW TO MAKE A SUNDIAL

Can you tell time without looking at the clock? Long before watches and iPhones, people have been able to know what time it is. How? Some people could look at the position of the sun in the sky and guess the time of day. But others found a better way: sundials.

Sundials use a straight stick (called a "gnomon") to cast a shadow on a number that identifies what time it is. Sundials were used even in Old Testament times. The Bible mentions sundials in Isaiah 38:8: " 'Behold, I [the Lord] will make the shadow cast by the declining sun on the dial of Ahaz turn back ten steps.' So the sun turned back on the dial the ten steps by which it had declined."

What power or technology enables sundials to work? God! The universe, which God created, always runs precisely on schedule. The sun comes up and goes down according to the pattern he sets. You can set your watch by it. And using sundials, that is exactly what people have done for thousands of years. Here's how you can make a simple sundial.

What you will need: one piece of stiff cardboard (at least 18-inches wide and 24-inches long), one brand-new pencil (or a straight 7-inch stick), a protractor, a magnetic compass (or compass app), a pencil, a watch, and some tape.

1. Attach the pencil to the cardboard so it stands straight up. The pencil is your sundial's gnomon. The pencil should be centered on one side of the cardboard about 1 inch from the edge. You can attach the pencil by poking it through a small hole in the cardboard and then securing it in place with tape. Be sure the pencil isn't sticking out underneath the cardboard.

2. Use the protractor to make sure that the pencil is standing perfectly straight and not leaning to one side or the other. Rotating the protractor around all sides of the pencil, make sure that all sides of the pencil line up with the 90° mark on the protractor. If the pencil moves at all, add more tape to secure it so that it stays upright.

Turn the page for more directions

3. Place the cardboard in a sunny spot. Adjust it so that the edge of the cardboard opposite from the pencil faces north. You can use a real compass or a compass app to determine which direction is north. (You will also need to mark on the ground exactly where you've positioned the sundial. If it moves from its original spot, the sundial won't work properly.)

4. Look at your clock. When a new hour begins (for example, 4:00 in the afternoon), mark the cardboard to show where the shadow of the pencil fell at that exact time. Write the time next to the mark.

5. Repeat step #4 when each new hour begins, marking the shadow's new place every 60 minutes. Do this for several days to make sure your marks are in the right spots. Obviously, sundials only show daylight hours; so you will have to do your work between about 6:00 a.m. and 6:00 p.m.

6. Be very careful that the cardboard **does not move at all**. Secure the cardboard to the ground, or just mark the precise place where the cardboard is supposed to sit, so you can put it back in exactly the same sunny place later.

With your sundial you can tell time like ancient people did for thousands of years! And every time you look at the time, remember Psalm 104:19. (A good verse to write on the cardboard base of your sundial.)

64

MORE WOMEN WHO GAVE THEIR LIVES FOR CHRIST

SARAH EDWARDS

In 1710, James and Mary Pierpont welcomed a new daughter, Sarah, into their family in New Haven, Connecticut. Both James and Mary were devoted Christians; they were also well-educated and wealthy members of society in the early American colonies. James was a minister and one of the founders of Yale College (now Yale University). And Mary's grandfather had been the first mayor of New York City.

Not much is known of Sarah's childhood, but by the age of 13, she had begun to attract the attention of a smart, serious, and somewhat socially awkward student at Yale: Jonathan Edwards. (Spiritual, humble, intense, and brilliant, Edwards went on to become a famous pastor and is considered America's greatest theologian. The writings of this godly man are still widely read today.) Soon after meeting Sarah he wrote:

They say there is a young lady in [New Haven] who is beloved of that almighty Being, who made and rules the world, and that there are certain seasons in which this great Being, in some way or other invisible, comes to her and fills her mind with exceeding sweet delight, and that she hardly cares for anything, except to meditate on him.

Four years later, on July 28, 1727, Jonathan and Sarah were married. She was 17 and he was 23, five months into his new job as assistant pastor under his grandfather in Northampton, Massachusetts. Within two years his grandfather had died, and Jonathan became the senior pastor of the church.

Life married to Jonathan Edwards proved challenging and rewarding. Jonathan was a loving and tender father and husband, who made time for his wife and (eventually 11!) children. Yet most days he spent 14 hours in his study: preparing messages, praying for the church's 620 members, and counseling those who came to him for advice. Thus, while Sarah was free to interrupt Jonathan's schedule at any time, she was in charge of the daily business of their ever-growing household. Her everyday life was full of hard work—very different from the wealthy society in which she had grown up. One author has described the Edwards' household this way:

In our centrally-heated houses, it's difficult to imagine the tasks that were Sarah's to do or delegate: breaking ice to haul water, bringing in firewood and tending the fire, cooking and packing lunches for visiting travelers, making the family's clothing (from sheep-shearing through spinning and weaving to sewing), growing and preserving produce, making brooms, doing laundry, tending babies and nursing illnesses, making candles, feeding poultry, overseeing butchering, teaching the boys whatever they didn't learn at school, and seeing that the girls learned homemaking creativity. And that was only a fraction of Sarah's responsibilities.

And over time, all of Sarah's daily efforts in life and family blossomed in ways she never could have imagined. Their eleven children would go on to make important contributions to society. A study conducted in 1900 showed that, up until then, among their descendants there had been 13 college presidents, 65 professors, 100 lawyers, 30 judges, 66 physicians, and 80 holders of public office, including three US Senators, three mayors, three state governors, one US vice president, and one controller of the US Treasury.

Scripture Says

"Who is to condemn? Christ Jesus is the one who died—more than that, who was raised—who is at the right hand of God, who indeed is interceding for us." (Romans 8:34)

Read Sarah's own thoughts about Romans 8:34:

When I was alone, the words [of this verse] came to my mind with far greater power and sweetness; upon which I took the Bible, and read the words to the end of the chapter, when they were impressed on my heart with vastly greater power and sweetness still. . . . Melted and overcome by the sweetness of this assurance, I fell into a great flow of tears, and could not forbear weeping aloud. It appeared certain to me that God was my Father, and Christ my Lord and Savior, that he was mine and I his. . . . The presence of God was so near, and so real, that I seemed scarcely conscious of any thing else.

In addition, many had entered the ministry, and 100 others had served as overseas missionaries.

How could one woman do so much, so faithfully? The answer is that Sarah found strength by relying on her heavenly Father. Although very busy around the house, about the church, and in the lives of her 11 children, Sarah did not neglect her relationship with Christ. She pursued joy in God. One of her earliest biographers writes, "Her religion had nothing gloomy or forbidding in its character. Unusual as it was in degree, it was eminently the religion of joy."

After 23 years at the church in Northampton, the Edwards family left and became missionaries to the Indians in western Massachusetts. In this new area, without the pressures of leading a church, Jonathan devoted himself to writing, while Sarah, her children now older, spent more time enjoying her family. Seven years later, Jonathan was elected president of what was to become Princeton University.

Unknown to Sarah or Jonathan, this move to Princeton would begin the final chapter of their married lives. Jonathan had traveled alone to Princeton, New Jersey, with his family scheduled to follow in a few months' time. Only a few weeks after arriving at his new post, Jonathan contracted smallpox after being inoculated against the disease. He died a few days later. Sarah and the children were devastated at the loss. Yet God gave them strength to set their hope on the God who never dies. When Sarah heard the news, she immediately wrote to their grown daughter, Esther:

O my very Dear Child,

What shall I say. A holy and good God has covered us with a dark cloud. O that we may all kiss the rod and lay our hands on our mouths. The Lord has done it. He has made me adore his goodness that we had him so long. But my God lives and he has my heart. O what a legacy my husband and your father has left us. We are all given to God and there I am and love to be.

Your affectionate mother,
Sarah Edwards

But her daughter Esther never received this letter because she died on April 7, 1758. In October of that same year, Sarah herself died of rheumatic fever. She was only 49 years old.

Yet through the words of her own mouth and the generations that would live after her, Sarah's legacy would endure. She was a devoted mother, a wife, and church member. Yet none of these roles—wife, mother, church member, missionary—was most important to Sarah. At heart, Sarah Pierpont Edwards was a beloved child and joyful worshiper of her heavenly Father through the gospel of her Savior, Jesus Christ.

HANNA FAUST

Affectionately known as "Aunt Hanna" among German Christians, Johanna (shortened to Hanna) Faust is relatively unknown today in English-speaking countries. She wasn't a pastor's wife or a missionary. She wasn't an author or an athlete. She wasn't a genius, and she didn't come from an amazing family. She was simply a servant of Christ.

For over 60 years Hanna Faust helped those in need—the sick, the poor, the hurting, the sinful. As she tried to relieve the pain of others, she herself experienced great suffering. But earthly difficulty mattered little to Hanna in comparison with a person's eternal suffering. For alongside her labors of love came the message of Christ's love. She served for Christ and spoke of Christ.

Born in September 1825, Hanna grew up in Elberfeld, a village in the city of Wuppertal in northwestern Germany, not far from the Netherlands border. As a young girl, she spent long days weaving cloth in a mill. Yet in the early hours before work, she went to the river to wash clothes for sick people. After work, she spent evenings visiting the sick and the poor. One man described her activities, saying: "She would sweep chambers, make beds and, armed with pail and scrubbing brush, invade and clean the frowsiest [shabbiest] homes."

In the 1840s, when many German men and women were dying from cholera, Hanna continued to serve, even though she too began to develop symptoms of the disease. She said, "You cannot really take me away from my poor sick ones; they need me too sorely." And through all this, God protected her. She recalled, "In typhus, in cholera, in black smallpox I nursed [others to health] day and night and was preserved safely. Once when I had not undressed for three weeks, I went to Kronenburg [2 hours away] and slept 18 hours. Then I returned, fresh and happy, to Elberfeld."

As an adult, the burden of Hanna's difficulties became even heavier. Sadly, her husband was often drunk, and

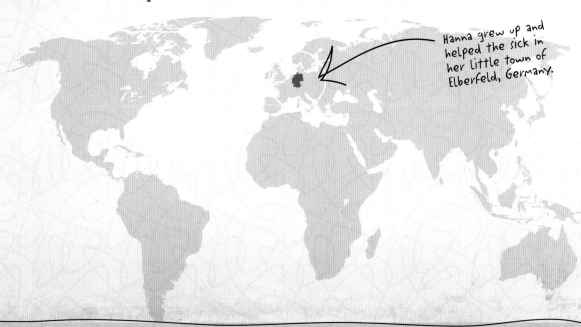

Hanna grew up and helped the sick in her little town of Elberfeld, Germany.

although she no longer worked as a weaver, she now earned a small income by selling coffee along the streets of her town, carrying a heavy basket of coffee on each arm. This meant that she struggled to earn enough money to pay for basic needs. Her clothes were rough (because that kind of cloth was cheapest) and threadbare (because she didn't buy new clothes when the old ones became worn). Her daily diet often included only the simplest food—grain, soup, potatoes, and milk.

Yet as she suffered and helped others who suffered, she maintained her sense of humor and beamed with joy. Once a wealthy businessman expressed surprise at her good attitude: "Frau [German for "Mrs."] Faust, how happy you look!" Hanna replied by telling the man about the peace and joy she found in Jesus, adding: "You can be just as happy."

Her journeys around town brought her into contact with the lowest of society: the outcasts and the criminals. For these she collected and distributed money, clothing, and food. Over time she founded several associations to promote this kind of help. She also started a Sunday school for children in the worst part of town, a slum called Elendstal. It was here that the children gave her the name by which she became known: Aunt Hanna.

Hanna lived until 1903. Even in old age, Aunt Hanna gave herself, like Jesus, to serve others. Into her 70s, she visited prisons and helped girls who lived on the streets. Sometimes, on the streets of Elberfeld she also found her life in danger. Once, she arrived home to find a mob outside her house. At the center of the crowd, a son was about to stab his own father with a knife. Hanna reached out, grabbed the son's arm, stopped the fight, and led him home. Another time, Hanna boldly entered a broken down house to stop a husband from attacking his wife with an ax. Her courage and kindness were legendary.

So, why did Hanna—a regular woman—give her life to serve others? Hanna gave herself for others because Christ had first given himself for her. Remembering times of suffering, Hanna said, "In these years my Savior became all to me." For it was as a young girl, Hanna had turned to Christ to save her from sin. She also served because she wanted people to hear the good news about Jesus. She was convinced that people would understand the Word of God more clearly when they had "seen" its invisible truth through visible service. She said, "You've got to show the people you love them, and then you'll win them."

Hanna Faust was an ordinary woman. Yet she accomplished extraordinary things by giving herself in lowly service for her exalted Savior.

MORE TO
EXPLORE

If you'd like to learn about other godly women, you may want to read these books from Janet and Geoff Benge's "Christian Heroes Then & Now" Series: *Mary Slessor: Forward into Calabar* and *Elisabeth Elliot: Joyful Surrender*.

65

WEAPONS IN THE BIBLE

FOR WE ARE NOT FIGHTING AGAINST FLESH-AND-BLOOD ENEMIES, BUT AGAINST EVIL RULERS AND AUTHORITIES OF THE UNSEEN WORLD, AGAINST MIGHTY POWERS IN THIS DARK WORLD, AND AGAINST EVIL SPIRITS IN THE HEAVENLY PLACES.
EPHESIANS 6:12 NLT

The Bible is packed with tales of warfare. Its pages recount grueling sieges, savage duels, open combat, and secret plans. Even God himself fights for his people as a divine warrior (Habakkuk 3:3–15). In fact, the Bible itself is called the "sword" of the Spirit (Ephesians 6:17).

From the very beginning, God said that because of sin this world would be filled with fighting. Ever since Adam and Eve gave in to Satan's temptations, there has been spiritual conflict between God's people and those who belong to Satan (Genesis 3:15).

Jesus said, "If the world hates you, know that it has hated me before it hated you" (John 15:18). God's people have always been engaged in this kind of conflict.

Yet in the New Testament, the followers of Christ do not pick up sword and shield to fight physical enemies. Instead, they are engaged in *spiritual* warfare (Ephesians 6:10–17). Those who belong to Christ fight spiritual battles knowing that the war has already been won. By his death and resurrection, Jesus defeated death, sin, and the devil. (Verses to read: John 16:11; Colossians 3:15; Hebrews 2:14.)

How many Roman guards did Paul have at one time?
470 guards (Acts 23:23)

However back in Old Testament times, the battles fought by God's people were often actual battles fought with deadly weapons. Here are some of the weapons mentioned in the Bible:

BATTLE-AX. Used in hand-to-hand combat, this weapon was designed to crush or shatter (Jeremiah 51:20). Smaller versions of this giant hammer included "rods," which were stout wooden staffs, often weighted at one end for maximum impact (Psalm 2:9 and 23:4).

SPEAR. This throwing weapon of the common soldier was a long wooden shaft tipped with a head of metal (1 Samuel 17:6-7). It was similar to the javelin (Job 41:26).

BOW AND ARROW. Made of wood and often reinforced with bronze or animal horn or sinew, bows were a common weapon in ancient times (Jeremiah 50:14; 1 Chronicles 5:18). Archers on foot or horseback used single- or double-curve bows to launch arrows made of reeds, sometimes tipped with metal heads.

SWORD. By far the most common weapon mentioned in the Bible is the sword (423 times!). But not all swords are the same.

SICKLE SWORD—made of a single piece of curved metal, this sword helped the Israelites conquer the land of Canaan around 1406 B.C.

BROAD SWORD—carried in a sheath, which hung from a belt, this weapon was straight and longer than the sickle sword. This gave greater power in striking. As introduced by the Philistines, the broad sword at first had only a single edge (Judges 1:8). Later developments added a second edge, a "double-edged sword" (Revelation 2:12).

SHORT SWORD—a short sword or dagger became the regular side arm of the Roman soldier (Ephesians 6:17; Luke 22:52). But hundreds of years before, an Israelite judge, Ehud, used a dagger to kill wicked king Eglon (Judges 3:21). Soldiers did not hack with the edge of this blade, but instead used its point to jab at the enemy.

SLING. This long-range weapon was used both by shepherds and also by soldiers (1 Samuel 17:40). (See page 42 for more about slings.)

CATAPULT. A massive, later upgrade of the sling was the catapult (2 Chronicles 26:15), the most feared weapon from 800 B.C. to A.D. 1500. More advanced models of ancient catapults could sling boulders weighing several tons the length of four football fields!

How much did the giant Goliath's armor weigh?

About 125 pounds (1 Samuel 17:5)

MAKE YOUR OWN CATAPULT

What You'll Need: eight tongue depressors, at least three sturdy rubber bands, a soda bottle cap, and a glue gun or glue.

1. Wrap two tongue depressors together with a rubber band at one end.

2. Stack six tongue depressors and slide the group in between the two connected tongue depressors so the two sticks open up.

3. Use two rubber bands to firmly attach the two sets of tongue depressors together where they connect. First attach one on the diagonal and then the second one on the other diagonal.

4. Use a hot glue gun (or regular glue) to secure the soda bottle cap to the far end of one of the two opened-up tongue depressors.

5. Give it time to dry. Now the catapult is ready to use. Place what you are launching into the soda cap, push down on the end, and release. Remember: launch in a safe direction, and wear safety glasses. Indoors, launch soft items like marshmallows or erasers.

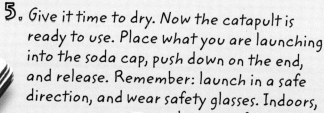

66

CHRISTIAN SYMBOLS YOU SHOULD KNOW

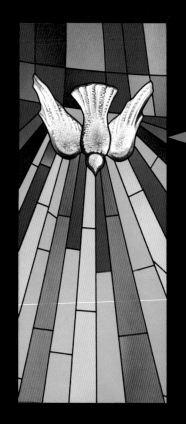

1

2

3

4

1 **ALPHA/OMEGA**—*Alpha* (A) is the first letter of the Greek alphabet, and *omega* (Ω) is the last. (See page 200 to learn more about Greek.) In the last book of the Bible, Jesus says, "I am the Alpha and the Omega, the beginning and the ending" (Revelation 1:8; 21:6; 22:13). The A/Ω symbol reminds us that no matter what happens to us, Jesus is always with us, from start to finish.

2 **ANCHOR**—The anchor reminds us that Jesus keeps us stable and secure. This is how Hebrews 6:19-20 speaks about our confident hope in Jesus. Our hope is anchored in heaven, so all Christians (those connected to Jesus), will one day arrive safely into the harbor of heaven as well.

3 **DOVE**—In the Bible, the Holy Spirit is sometimes represented by a bird or dove. In Genesis 1:2, the Holy Spirit hovers over the waters like a mother bird, tenderly nurturing creation. At Jesus's baptism, the Holy Spirit descends in the form of a dove, the symbol of peace (Matthew 3:16).

4 **CHI-RHO**—The first two letters in the Greek name for Christ are a *chi* (X) and a *rho* (P). Early Christians combined these letters to create a symbol that reminded them of the Savior, Jesus Christ.

Turn the page for more symbols ——————————→

Did You KNOW ?

The universal symbol of Christianity is not the manger of the baby, nor the hammer of the carpenter's son, neither is it the towel of the divine servant. The symbol of Christ and his church is simply the cross, pointing not to his birth, his teaching, nor to his miracles or his resurrection. But instead, to the cross, which stands as a reminder of his humble and painful death in our place and for our sin (paraphrased from John Stott's *The Cross of Christ*).

5 CROSS—In Jesus's day, the Roman Empire used the cross to execute the worst of criminals. Yet because Jesus died on a cross in punishment of sin, this awful tool of death now represents the Good News about Jesus's sacrifice for sinners.

6 FISH—This symbol is known by the Greek name for fish, the ΙΧΘΥΣ (*ichthus*). This reminds us that Jesus called his disciples with these words: "Follow me, and I will make you become fishers of men" (Mark 1:17). But the letters in this Greek word also form an acrostic: each letter of ΙΧΘΥΣ stands for an entire word or name.

Iota (Ι) is the first letter of "Jesus"; chi (Χ) is the first letter in "Christ"; theta (Θ) is the first letter in "God"; upsilon (Υ) is the first letter in "Son"; and sigma (Σ) is the first letter in "Savior."

7 TRIANGLE—Christians used this three-sided symbol to point to the three members of the Godhead: Father, Son, and Spirit. Sometimes Christians drew a simple triangle, others came up with more beautiful and complicated versions. The words in this image are in Latin. See if you can figure out what they say.

67

WHAT TO DO WHEN BAD THINGS HAPPEN

"There *was* a real railway accident," said Aslan softly. "Your father and mother and all of you are—as you used to call it in the Shadow-Lands—dead."
C. S. Lewis, *The Last Battle*

With these words, C. S. Lewis begins the ending of the final book in *The Chronicles of Narnia*. The heroes in the story hear the awful news that announces their own pain and loss. And these children are not alone in experiencing hardship. At some time in *your* life, your parents have probably taken you to the emergency room. You may also have moved away from friends, lost a favorite toy or pet, or even worse. It's easy to enjoy the good things in life, but how should you respond when bad things happen?

Jesus knows exactly what we need to do. Why? Because he knows exactly what you are going through. After all, he came down to earth and suffered and died (Isaiah 53:4–6). God himself has experienced your pain. And here's what he says to do when facing bad and difficult things:

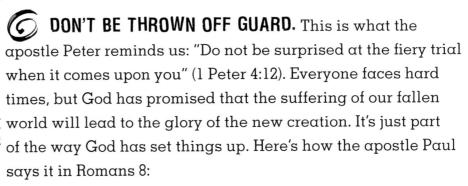

DON'T BE THROWN OFF GUARD. This is what the apostle Peter reminds us: "Do not be surprised at the fiery trial when it comes upon you" (1 Peter 4:12). Everyone faces hard times, but God has promised that the suffering of our fallen world will lead to the glory of the new creation. It's just part of the way God has set things up. Here's how the apostle Paul says it in Romans 8:

For we know that all creation has been groaning as in the pains of childbirth right up to the present time. And we believers also groan, even though we have the Holy Spirit within us as a foretaste of future glory, for we long for our bodies to be released from sin and suffering. We, too, wait with eager hope for the day when God will give us our full rights as his adopted children, including the new bodies he has promised us. (Romans 8:22–23 NLT)

TELL GOD HOW YOU FEEL. When bad things happen, God doesn't want you to bottle up all your pain inside your heart. You should tell others how you feel. He also wants you to express your hurt, anger, and sadness to him. Even if you don't know the words to say, the Holy Spirit listens to your groaning heart and prays to the Father for you.

God's Spirit is right alongside helping us along. If we don't know how or what to pray, it doesn't matter. He does our praying in and for us, making prayer out of our wordless sighs, our aching groans. He knows us far better than we know ourselves, knows our . . . condition, and keeps us present before God. (Romans 8:26b–27 The Message)

⟳ TRUST IN GOD'S GOOD PLAN.

God has a master plan for your life. He is orchestrating everything that happens to you for a purpose: to make you more like his Son, Jesus Christ. God uses pain to shape believers to be more like Christ.

That's why we can be so sure that every detail in our lives of love for God is worked into something good. God knew what he was doing from the very beginning. He decided from the outset to shape the lives of those who love him along the same lines as the life of his Son. The Son stands first

THINK ABOUT IT

One of the most famous Christians of the 1800s was British pastor Charles Spurgeon (1834–1892). A brilliant preacher who loved the gospel of Christ, he was known for having a lively sense of humor. Yet he suffered more than most people. Though loved by many for his gospel ministry, he was also greatly  hated by others for the same reason. He struggled with fear and depression. He also carried the burdens of an enormous workload and the intense pain that comes from a disease of the joints called gout. But through all the stormy waves that crashed against him, Spurgeon could bless the Lord. He said, "I have learned to kiss the wave that throws me against the Rock of Ages."

in the line of humanity he restored. We see the original and intended shape of our lives there in him. (Romans 8:28–29 The Message)

⊙ REMEMBER WHOSE YOU ARE. In times of pain or sadness, it's easy to forget what God has done for you. Before you became a Christian, you were a lost sinner, doomed to face God's punishment for your sin. But now, as one of God's children, you are deeply loved—a member of his own family, forgiven, accepted, and treasured. The first part of Romans 8:30 teaches us that as Christians, no suffering can shake our relationship with God.

After God made that decision of what his children should be like, he followed it up by calling people by name. After he called them by name, he set them on a solid basis with himself. (Romans 8:30a The Message)

⊙ IMAGINE YOUR FUTURE. When you're suffering, it's hard to think about anything else. Yet God reminds us that even in our darkest moments, a bright future lies before every member of his family. The story of your life may contain many pages written in pain, but you know the "glory" of the Final Chapter— Christians are guaranteed joy with God forever.

And then, after getting them established, he stayed with them to the end, gloriously completing what he had begun. So, what do you think? With God on our side like this, how can we lose? If God didn't hesitate to put everything on the line for us, embracing our condition and exposing himself to the worst by sending his own Son, is there anything else he wouldn't gladly and freely do for us? (Romans 8:30b–32 The Message)

❦ ❦ ❦

In the *Chronicles of Narnia,* the children within the story faced pain and even worse—death. But for them, as for all who follow Jesus, that did not mean the end. Here's how the Narnia stories conclude:

> [Aslan said,] "The term is over: the holidays have begun. The dream is ended: this is the morning." And as He spoke He no longer looked to them like a lion; but the things that began to happen after that were so great and beautiful that I cannot write them. And for us this is the end of all the stories, and we can most truly say that they all lived happily ever after. But for them it was only the beginning of the real story. All their life in this world and all their adventures in Narnia had only been the cover and the title page: now at last they were beginning Chapter One of the Great Story, which no one on earth has read: which goes on for ever: in which every chapter is better than the one before. *(The Last Battle)*

HOW TO FIND ANYTHING IN THIS BOOK

HOW TO FIND ANYTHING IN THIS BOOK

Skills to Learn

Understanding the Bible

Acknowledgments

I am grateful for the kind collaboration of many over the last few years. Some chapter ideas were suggested by friends, family, and ministry colleagues: Jon Boulet, Jeff Bracht, Chris Brauns, Jim Hamilton, Andy Henderson, Matthew Hoskinson, Barbara Juliani, Will Lohnes, Marty Machowski, Jonathan Matias, Jeremy McMorris, Chris Morris, Dave Schutter, Eric Sipe, Brett Star, Darcy Stelzer, Mat Stribling, and Marty Sweeney.

Dr. Michael Barrett, Dr. Chris Brauns, Dr. Curtis Hill, Pastor Marty Machowski, my wife, Robben, and my sister Jenny, all read and provided valuable feedback and encouragement on an early draft. Seth Asher, Dan Boulet, Evan Collier, Dr. Mark Gignilliat, Dr. Blake Hardcastle, Robin Johnston, John Mason, Connor Pitman, and Patti Spencer also contributed helpful input on various chapters. Later versions received incalculable benefit through the expert and patient editorial guidance of New Growth Press's Nancy Winter and Barbara Juliani. Of course, I also want to recognize my eleven-year-old son, Micah, who read dad's book, gave great ideas, and prevented obvious, embarrassing mistakes. Additionally, I can't say enough about Scot McDonald's fantastic design. His creative energies brought all the fun-factor I had hoped for, and then some. *The Radical Book for Kids* is dedicated to my friend and former colleague, Shannon Brown, who through many projects and countless conversations has been a source of true encouragement to me: in writing, in godliness, and in life.

Most of all, I thank the Lord for the opportunity and strength to work on this project over the last few years. I pray that through these pages, many in the next generation will grow to love, trust, and reflect our gracious Savior more and more.

Endnotes

4   Chapter 1. Quotation from Michael Williams in Dane Ortlund's "What's the Message of the Bible in One Sentence" (http://dogmadoxa.blogspot.com/2011/01/whats-message-of-bible-in-one-sentence.html, accessed 20 May 2016).

12–15   Chapter 4. Concepts based on Timothy Keller's sermon at the 2007 Gospel Coalition conference.

17–18   Chapter 5. Quotation from Donald Whitney, *Spiritual Disciplines for the Christian Life* (Colorado Springs: NavPress, 1991) 17.

18   Chapter 5. Quotation about Charles Simeon in Handley Carr Glyn Moule, *Charles Simeon* (London: Methuen & Co., 1892), 45.

19   Chapter 6. Quotations from Polycarp, "The Epistle of Polycarp," *The Apostolic Fathers,* Part II, Vol. 3, ed. J. B. Lightfoot, 2nd ed. (London: Macmillan, 1889), 474 and 326.

20–21   Chapter 6. Quotations from Athanasius in Scot McKnight, *A Community Called Atonement* (Nashville: Abingdon Press, 2007), 54. And from *Programs and Sermons for Spiritual Instruction* (Dublin: Browne & Nolan, 1881), 112.

23   Chapter 6. Quotations from Augustine in *Saint Augustine: Confessions,* trans. Henry Chadwick (New York: Oxford University Press, Inc., 2008), 3, 52, 96, 152–3, 202.

28   Chapter 7. McCall, Bruce, "The Perfect Non-Apology Apology," *The New York Times* (New York), 22 April 2002.

35   Chapter 10. New Testament manuscript statistics taken from the online database provided at the New Testament Virtual Manuscript Room (http://ntvmr.uni-muenster.de/liste, accessed 19 April 2016).

37   Chapter 10. The translation of John 18:31–33; 37–38 (https://en.wikipedia.org/wiki/Rylands_Library_Papyrus_P52, accessed 20 May 2016).

44–46   Chapter 13. Quotations from J. C. Ryle, *Thoughts for Young Men* (Carlisle, PA: Banner of Truth, 2015, originally published in 1888).

45   Chapter 13. [box] Jim Elliot, *The Journal of Jim Elliot,* ed. Elisabeth Elliot (Grand Rapids: Revell, 1978), 174.

47   Chapter 14. Barna Study: Six Trends for 2014 (from https://www.barna.org/barna-update/culture/664-the-state-of-the-bible-6-trends-for-2014#.VXrlUM7UQ1E, accessed June 12, 2015)

73   Chapter 19. [box] from David A. Dorsey, *The Roads and Highways of Ancient Israel* (Baltimore: Johns Hopkins University Press, 1991), 1–24.

74   Chapter 19. Mileage table based on John H. Walton, *Chronological and Background Charts of the Old Testament* (Grand Rapids: Zondervan, 1994), 116.

78   Chapter 20. Quotation from John Piper (http://www.desiringgod.org/messages/god-is-most-glorified-in-us-when-we-are-most-satisfied-in-him, accessed 20 May 2016).

86   Chapter 23. Quotation from David Livingstone in Christopher J. H. Wright, *Knowing Jesus Through the Old Testament,* 2nd ed. (Downers Grove, IL: IVP, 2014), 137.

86   Chapter 23. Quotation from William Carey in Eustace Carey, *Memoir of William Carey, D.D.* (London: Jackson and Walford, 1836), 75.

88   Chapter 23. List at bottom of page adapted from David Hosaflook. Used by permission, personal correspondence with author.

91   Chapter 24. Quotation from Amy Carmichael in M. David Sills, *The Missionary Call: Find Your Place in God's Plan for the World* (Chicago: Moody Press, 2008), 191.

92   Chapter 24. Amy Carmichael, *If* (Fort Washington, PA: CLC Publications, 2011), 52.

93–94   Chapter 24. Quotations from Lottie Moon in *Send the Light: Lottie Moon's Letters and Other Writings,* ed. Keith Harper (Macon, GA: Mercer University Press, 2002), 132 & 239–40. Final quotation from the International Mission Board website (http://www.imb.org/main/lottie-moon/details.asp?StoryID=11887&LanguageID=1709#.Vz8ylGYtVUQ, accessed 20 May 2016).

103   Chapter 27. Martyn Lloyd-Jones, *Studies in the Sermon on the Mount* (Grand Rapids: Eerdmans, 2000), 244.

123–129   Chapter 32. Adapted from unpublished material written by the author, © Positive Action for Christ, PO Box 700, Whitakers, NC 27891. All rights reserved. Used by special permission.

125   Chapter 32. J. I. Packer, *Knowing God* (Downers Grove, IL: IVP, 1973), 26.

133–134   Chapter 33. From Don Richardson, *Eternity in Their Hearts* (Grand Rapids: Baker, 1981), 57, 74, 115, 128f.

133   Chapter 33. C. S. Lewis, *The Weight of Glory and Other Addresses* (New York: Harper Collins, 1980), 140.

137   Chapter 34. In item #3, the analogy of the fireplace is adapted from Jim Berg, *Changed Into His Image* (Greenville, SC: BJU Press, 1999), 93.

137   Chapter 34. Boice quotation from *Give Praise to God,* Philip G. Ryken, et al, eds. (Phillipsburg, NJ: P&R Publishing, 2011), 233.

145   Chapter 36. The graphic of clean and unclean foods adapted and used with permission from Mark Barry (https://visualunit.me/2014/11/02/a-guide-to-unclean-eating/, accessed 20 May 2016).

147   Chapter 37. Quotation from John Huss in Matthew Spinka, *John Hus: Doctrine of the Church* (Princeton, NJ: Princeton University Press, 1966), 161, 320. Final quotation from http://www.baptistboard.com/threads/an-address-to-his-persecutors-and-a-prayer-to-god.95783/, accessed 20 May 2016.

149   Chapter 37. Martin Luther, *Larger Catechism,* trans. John Nicholas Lenker (Minneapolis, MN: Luther Press, 1908), 44. The final quote is attributed to Luther, for similar see Paul Althaus, *The Theology of Martin Luther,* trans. Robert C. Schultz (Philadelphia: Fortress Press, 1966), 246.

151   Chapter 37. Quotations of Martin Luther from Roland Bainton, *Here I Stand: A Life of Martin Luther* (Peabody, MA: Hendrickson, 2009), 180.

152   Chapter 37. Quotations from John Bunyan in *The Whole Works of John Bunyan,* ed. George Offor, Vol. 1 (London: Blackie and Son, 1862), cxvi & 486.

152   Chapter 37. John Bunyan, *Grace Abounding to the Chief of Sinners* (New York: Penguin Group, 1987), 34–5.

153   Chapter 37. Joseph Ivimey, *The Life of Mr. John Bunyan* (London: R. Edwards: London, 1809), 225, 332.

158–159   Chapter 40. Adapted from unpublished material written by the author, © Positive Action for Christ, P.O. Box 700, Whitakers, NC 27891. All rights reserved. Used by special permission.

159   Chapter 40. Quotation from Martin Luther in *Luther's Small Catechism,* (Philadelphia: Lutheran Publication Society, 1893), 17.

166   Chapter 42. Malcolm W. Browne, "Following Benford's Law, or Looking Out for No. 1" (*The New York Times,* Tuesday, August 4, 1998).

167   Chapter 42. Martin Rees, *Just Six Numbers: The Deep Forces that Shape the Universe* (New York: Basic Books, 2000), 30.

164–167   Chapter 42. Adapted from unpublished material written by the author, © Positive Action for Christ, P.O. Box 700, Whitakers, NC 27891. All rights reserved. Used by special permission.

169   Chapter 43. Martin Luther, *A Simple Way to Pray* (Louisville, KY: Westminster John Knox Press, 2000), 32–3.

172–174   Chapter 44. Adapted from article written by the author and printed with permission from *Today's Christian Teen* magazine.

176   Chapter 45. Michael Reeves, *Delighting in the Trinity: An Introduction to the Christian Faith* (Downers Grove, IL: IVP, 2012), 31.

180   Chapter 45. "His Robes for Mine" © ChurchWorks Media.com, 2008.

183   Chapter 46. Quotations from *The Collected Letters of C.S. Lewis, Vol. II: Family Letters 1905–1931* (New York: Harper Collins, 2004), 174.

183   Chapter 46. Quotations from C. S. Lewis, *The Four Loves* (Orlando, FL: Harcourt Books, 1971), 66–7.

201   Chapter 52. Adapted from unpublished material written by the author, © Positive Action for Christ, P. O. Box 700, Whitakers, NC 27891. All rights reserved. Used by special permission.

212–213   Chapter 56. Dimensional descriptors adapted from John Stott, *The Incomparable Christ* (Downers Grove, IL: IVP, 2001), 41–2.

223   Chapter 60. Letter of Pliny to Trajan from *A Dictionary of the Bible,* ed. James Hastings, Vol. 4 (New York: Charles Scribner's Sons, 1911), 943.

233–234   Chapter 64. Quotation from Iain H. Murray, *Jonathan Edwards: A New Biography* (Edinburgh: Banner of Truth, 1987), 92.

234–235   Chapter 64. Quotation from Noël Piper, *Faithful Women & Their Extraordinary God* (Wheaton, IL: Crossway, 2005), 23.

235   Chapter 64 [box]. Sereno Edwards, *The Life of President Edwards* (New York: Carvill, 1830), 173.

236   Ibid., 131.

237   Ibid., 580–1.

239–241   Chapter 64. Quotations from Ernest Gordon, *A Book of Protestant Saints* (Chicago: Moody, 1946), 305–6.

247   Chapter 66. Adapted from John Stott, *The Cross of Christ* (Downers Grove, IL: IVP, 1986), 21.

249   Chapter 67. C. S. Lewis, *The Last Battle* (New York: Macmillan, 1956), 173.

253   Ibid., 173–4.

Illustrations

ENDORSEMENTS FOR *THE RADICAL BOOK FOR KIDS*

"*The Radical Book for Kids* is like an encyclopedia of Truth. Thornton has done something magical here. He's taken every aspect of the Christian faith, the Word we love, and the character of God and made it accessible to children. It's everything you'd hope to know and teach in one place, even including stories of historical figures. I'm thankful my kids are still young, so I can use this book to teach them about the roots of our faith. *The Radical Book for Kids* is radical indeed—radically helpful, radically good."

—TRILLIA NEWBELL, Author of *Enjoy* (forthcoming, 2017), *Fear and Faith*, and *United*

"My wife and I only wish that this book had been available for our children and our grandchildren. It's difficult in a few words to express my appreciation for the attractive and absorbing way it engages the young readers it has in view by highlighting Scripture's pervasive focus on Christ and by showing the importance of the gospel and its implications for their lives. I commend it most highly."

—RICHARD B. GAFFIN, JR., Professor of Biblical and Systematic Theology, Emeritus, Westminster Theological Seminary

"Champ gives children and their parents a gift in this book that is fun, practical, and theologically rich. It is a necessary explorer's guide to the Bible, theology, biblical and church history, and life for boys and girls. It's a tool for children to learn about God, his Word, his world, and themselves."

—JUSTIN S. HOLCOMB, Seminary professor; minister; author of *God Made All of Me: A Book to Help Children Protect Their Bodies*

"As I paged through this book, I kept finding assorted facts and tips that never manage to make it into my Sunday school lessons or family devotions—but should! This is a wonder-filled book for kids to explore. They will learn, have fun, and be challenged to grow deeper in faith."

—JACK KLUMPENHOWER, Author of *Show Them Jesus*; coauthor of *The Gospel-Centered Parent* and *What's Up?*

"*The Radical Book for Kids* is like packaging that awesome Sunday school teacher you remember in a book. You know, she was the amazing mom who made learning about God a ton of fun but did it with gospel truth that transformed lives. Every family should have a copy of *The Radical Book for Kids* on their bookshelf—better yet, put it out like a plate of cookies on the coffee table and watch your kids devour it. The most exciting part of all will be seeing your children grow in their passion for God and his Word."

—MARTY MACHOWSKI, Family pastor; author of *The Ology, The Gospel Story Bible, Long Story Short*, and other gospel-rich resources for families

"I do not as a habit read books for children, at least I haven't for several years now. However, I found Champ Thorton's *The Radical Book for Kids* to live up to its name. It is unlike anything I remember reading to my children. The scope and content are indeed radically different than the normal storytelling style of so many others. Champ is able to communicate important and sometimes complicated matters in simple and attention-grapping ways. I would be happy if my graduate students would come to me with the foundational knowledge of some of the issues addressed."

—MICHAEL BARRETT, Vice President for Academic Affairs/Academic Dean; Professor of Old Testament, Puritan Reformed Theological Seminary

"*The Radical Book for Kids* is one book that every family should have in their library. I cannot wait to read it with my children and learn more from it myself. Champ Thornton masterfully weaves together theology, biography, biblical truths, practical application, and interesting activities all in a book that is visual appealing and easy to read. I recommend this book for youth, parents, and new believers of all ages—it is a treasure trove of biblical insight and understanding."

—MELISSA KRUGER, Women's Ministry Coordinator at Uptown Church PCA; author of *The Envy of Eve: Finding Contentment in a Covetous World* and *Walking with God in the Season of Motherhood*

"I have three daughters and I'm always on the lookout for solid books. Champ Thornton's *Radical Book* fits the bill. It was an instant hit with my kids! It's got great design, rich theology, and is written in language that kids get. It's a book you should have in your home."

—MATHEW B. SIMS, Writer and Freelance Editor; author of *A Household Gospel*; blogger at Grace for Sinners (RSS)

"Superheroes, beasts, enemies, a (not so) secret mission, the greatest love story! This book will shape for youth a big-God worldview and nurture Christ-exalting living. It's filled with fascinating nuggets, memorable bites, rich theology, clear wisdom, and fun ideas. The pictures and topics are varied and engaging and will both draw your child into God's world and Word and propel him or her toward maturity, responsibility, and godliness."

—JASON S. DEROUCHIE, Professor of Old Testament and Biblical Theology, Bethlehem College & Seminary

"Champ Thornton's book shows families how to grow a root system in the Christian faith. It offers a broad base of rich content in meal-sized portions readily accessible to families. The content ranges from an introduction to Scripture, to biblical theology, to historical theology. The elephant jokes and knot tying lessons are a nice bonus. I am putting this on a short list of books I recommend that all our church families own."

—CHRIS BRAUNS, Pastor; author of *Unpacking Forgiveness*

"*The Radical Book for Kids* is a book that every Christian child should own. Full of great insights, fun facts, and great activities, it is the perfect companion to help children unpack the Bible and their faith at a deeper level. We need to encourage our children to develop a love for the Bible that will help them to stand for the Lord in every area of their lives through the years. *The Radical Book for Kids* will help them to do just that!"

—OLLY GOLDENBERG, CHILDREN CAN, www.childrencan.co.uk

"Intriguing + edifying = the kind of book I want my kids reading. This is one of them."

—ANDY NASELLI, Assistant Professor of New Testament and Biblical Theology, Bethlehem College & Seminary

"Champ Thornton's *The Radical Book for Kids* is a wonderful presentation of core Christian truth and practice that stands out in both style and substance. I can immediately see many possible uses for this book, but I particularly commend it to parents as a fun way to talk about faith with their kids. There is a feel of randomness in the selections of the topics, but I think that adds to the attractiveness of the book. Highly recommended."

—STEPHEN SMALLMAN, Author of *The Walk-Steps for New* and *Renewed Followers of Jesus*

"*The Radical Book for Kids* is deceptively fun! While preteens are utterly enjoying themselves with the creative games, hands-on projects, laugh-out-loud jokes, and cool stories, Champ Thornton is radically discipling them with a crash course on Bible study methods, hermeneutics, church history, biblical theology, and Christian life and ethics. This is the kind of book that stealthily helps parents, pastors, and teachers make young followers for Jesus Christ."

—MATTHEW C. MITCHELL, Pastor of Lanse Evangelical Free Church; author of *Resisting Gossip: Winning the War of the Wagging Tongue*; father of four

"In *The Radical Book for Kids*, Champ Thornton brilliantly combines words, drawing vivid pictures in one's mind to simplify key spiritual truths. Every parent, grandparent, and spiritual influencer of kids will want a copy for themselves due to the depth, insight, and comprehensive knowledge provided all in one convenient book. Kids will totally relate to the cultural relevance, fun facts, historical heroes, clever illustrations, and hands-on applications provided throughout."

—DARCY STELZER, KidzLife Ministry Director, New Life Church, Gahanna, Ohio